Actions
Speak
Louder

exploring ways to leverage your position in the workplace to benefit everyone and diversify your assumptions about professionalism so you can unlock overlooked potential. It also examines tips for articulating the moral and business case for DEI to stakeholders so your allyship can be most effective.

Part II, "Organizational Development," zeros in on specific elements of DEI practice. It explores strategies for improving organizational operations like recruiting, hiring, onboarding, retention, mentoring, meetings, and performance reviews that maximize long-term DEI impact.

Vocabulary

Before exploring DEI practices and the internal work they entail, we need to better understand some basic principles of DEI. Social justice movements strive to create diversity, equity, and inclusion in all levels of society. Most public attention goes to those that focus on securing political power, legal protections, and economic investment for marginalized communities. For example, Black Lives Matter movements focus on police reform, Me Too movements concentrate on sexual harassment laws, and marriage equality movements seek constitutional rights for LGBTQ+ people.

In some ways, DEI differs from these larger movements. Whereas they focus on broad social issues, DEI focuses on issues related to the workplace. Of course, the line between the social and the professional blurs, but it tends to focus on issues like recruiting, hiring, onboarding, retaining, and mentoring people from underrepresented long for the days where clear lines divided what was personal from what was professional. But as the story of my family shows, for many these lines never existed. My great-great-grandfather couldn't keep his blackness a personal issue when he went to work. Uncle Buck couldn't keep social problems like segregation at home when he went into the office. DEI helps business leaders recognize how team members from marginalized communities inhabit a social space that inextricably links the personal and the professional.

In this book, readers will learn how to examine themselves and the professional realms they occupy. Through reflection exercises, they will explore their social identities and appreciate the social identities of others in ways that create a deeper sense of workplace belonging. They will challenge their culturally relative biases about what constitutes professionalism and learn tips for how to diversify their thinking. Narratives, case studies, and statistics, as well as personal exercises, will offer a detailed outline of the inclusive practices that earn support, minimize exhaustion, and maximize success.

While exploring how to create more inclusive spaces for marginalized communities, readers will also discover strategies that benefit everyone. Even those who don't have to worry about lynching or Jim Crow laws increasingly seek employers who know how to make work professionally rewarding as well as personally fulfilling and socially responsible. In this way, DEI becomes not only a moral and ethical issue but also an essential business practice for those who want to attract and retain the most innovative talent in the twenty-first century.

To achieve these tasks, *Actions Speak Louder* is divided into two parts.

Part I, "Personal Development," concentrates on self-examination,

States do so in the historical shadow of COLORED ONLY signs and photographs of smiling couples pointing up at bodies in the trees. Every time they hear another racist joke, witness another example of false equivalence, or read a coworker's insensitive social media post, they remember that any advancements Black people have made in the professional world have always teetered on the brink. Whenever they look at the roster of team photographs on a prospective employer's website and don't see a single face that looks like theirs, they have to garner the bravery to even interview for an organization where they'll be the only Black person in a sea of White people.

Numerous studies catalog the enormous toll this reality takes on Black professionals. When people belong to groups that have been persecuted, they receive innumerable little reminders of how dangerous their position is, producing a kind of anxiety that can alter their physiology. Constantly responding to the threat of being outnumbered, threatened, or unwelcome, they can experience damage on a cellular level. Racism kills through beatings, murders, and lynchings but also through RNA inflammation, hypertension, and stress. No matter how much they achieve, many resemble my uncle Buck and fear the mob is in the next conference room. Even if there is no horde trying to kill them, the historically justified fear that there might be is enough to become the thing that does. In short, the workplace is harmful to underrepresented employees, and organizations need to develop policies that acknowledge this reality. By bravely confronting the past and understanding the present, diversity, equity, and inclusion (DEI) can provide strategies that can make a better future for everyone.

This book is a step-by-step guide for making more inclusive workplaces where everyone can show up as their whole selves. Some exam he completed, every job promotion he earned, every directive he gave an employee, every day he showed up for work—he feared the mob was always waiting outside his office with a new rope.

History That Still Haunts Us

When I tell this story, most shake their heads in disbelief. When I tell it to Black professionals, however, most nod their heads in recognition. The former group feels shock, but the latter matches this story with ones from their family history marked with racial violence. Stories of an enterprising ancestor who faced a mob or of an ambitious grandparent cut down by terrorists aren't new to them. Every time they enter their place of business, some feel the suspicion that everything they've achieved could be snatched away in an instant just like it was for so many and continues to be for many more.

People want to believe the American dream invites everyone to aim high, but the reality is that the mob awaited African Americans who dreamed too big. Between 1882 and 1968, on average, a Black person was beaten, whipped, burned, hanged, and dismembered by a mob every nine days. Many of these instances of violence flared up against people like my great-great-grandfather, who committed no crime other than being industrious. For every great-great-grandfather who hung from a tree, there was an Uncle Buck who remained traumatized no matter how far they advanced. And for every Uncle Buck who advanced, there were countless others who learned that if they wished to survive, they shouldn't try at all.

Twenty-first-century Black Americans working in the United

next. Struggling to make sense of the gaps he left in the story, my mind fills in the blanks.

It imagines a mob of White men breaking into my great-great-grandfather's house in the middle of the night, wrenching him from his bed, and dragging him out into the night. In front of his family, they beat him within an inch of his life and tie a noose around his neck. On the property he had the audacity to buy with the fruits of the labor he thought were his, they hang him from a tree. I don't know if my great-uncle looked up at the body of his patriarch. All he said was his father figure was lynched for being entrepreneurial.

Before the moment Uncle Buck told me this story, we had known each other for thirty-seven years, and in all that time, he never even mentioned it. As far as I can tell, this is a tale only a few in my family have heard, because no one talks about it. In fact, the only reason Uncle Buck broke his silence was to warn me. There was no justice for my great-great-grandfather, and sitting at Uncle Buck's kitchen table, watching his gaze seem to peer through the wall, I could see how this story still haunted him.

Wanting to encourage him, I said he had made his grandfather proud. That little boy had been there and seen what happened to Black people who tried to create a profession, but he persevered. He had gone on to college, got a job with the government, and achieved extraordinary leadership positions, especially for a Black man in his time. Meeting my eyes, he said he might have attained what this country would call success, accomplished things his grandfather never could, and achieved things that whips, pyres, and nooses tried to keep Black people from doing. Still, every step of the way—every

Introduction

"A New Rope"

When I told my great-uncle Buck that I wanted to write this book, he smiled. But when I explained I wanted to explore strategies for overcoming inequality in the workplace, his smile faded. He questioned whether I was sure I wanted to look at how racism cut people down. When I asked what he meant, he took a deep sigh and told me this story.

After the end of slavery, my great-great-grandfather—his grandfather—started farming for himself in South Carolina. After a while, he figured out how to sell cotton for a profit and became the biggest seller to the county's Black community. Someone recommended he sell to Whites, but he knew conducting business across the color line was dangerous. Seeking to grow but wanting protections, he hatched a plan. He'd plant, cultivate, and harvest the product before giving it to a White man he'd hired to sell to customers who'd buy only from someone who looked like them. But once news spread about his arrangement, the town's White people retaliated.

My uncle Buck didn't provide many details about what happened

Contents

*Dedicated to Marion "Buck"
Seabrooks, Christine Seabrooks,
Josephine Ponder, Malkit Singh Gill,
and the many other ancestors
who built the bridges I stand on*

Portfolio / Penguin
An imprint of Penguin Random House LLC
penguinrandomhouse.com

Most Portfolio books are available at a discount when purchased in quantity for sales promotions or corporate use. Special editions, which include personalized covers, excerpts, and corporate imprints, can be created when purchased in large quantities. For more information, please call (212) 572-2232 or e-mail specialmarkets @penguinrandomhouse.com. Your local bookstore can also assist with discounted bulk purchases using the Penguin Random House corporate Business-to-Business program. For assistance in locating a participating retailer, e-mail B2B @penguinrandomhouse.com.

Library of Congress Cataloging-in-Publication Data
Names: Singh, Deanna, author.
Title: Actions speak louder : a step-by-step guide to becoming an inclusive
    workplace / Deanna Singh.
Description: First edition. | New York : Portfolio, [2022] | Includes
    bibliographical references and index.
Identifiers: LCCN 2021053958 (print) | LCCN 2021053959 (ebook) |
    ISBN 9780593418215 (hardcover) | ISBN 9780593418222 (ebook)
Subjects: LCSH: Diversity in the workplace. | Teams in the workplace. |
    Organizational change. | Leadership.
Classification: LCC HF5549.5.M5 S566 2022 (print) | LCC HF5549.5.M5 (ebook) |
    DDC 658.3008—dc23/eng/20211228
LC record available at https://lccn.loc.gov/2021053958
LC ebook record available at https://lccn.loc.gov/2021053959

Printed in the United States of America
1st Printing

Book design by Cassandra Garruzzo Mueller

Names and identifying characteristics have been changed to protect the privacy of the individuals involved.

Actions Speak Louder

A Step-by-Step Guide
to Becoming an
Inclusive Workplace

Deanna Singh

PORTFOLIO | PENGUIN

groups. Social justice movements might demand equality from political leaders by insisting it is the morally right thing to do. DEI often strives to show business leaders how inclusion is also the financially smart thing to do.

Within DEI, there are many core terms. Definitions for these concepts vary, but this book will use the following definitions.

Underrepresented groups: Social demographics that have a smaller percentage in the workplace than in larger society.

When discussing underrepresented groups, this book concentrates on social identities along the lines of categories like race, ethnicity, gender, gender identity, socioeconomic status, sexual orientation, age, national origin, ability status, and military status.

Social identity can lead to certain experiences that inform thinking. Industries that want new thinking can turn to new groups. For example, people of color, LGBTQ+ people, non-Christians, first-generation professionals, immigrants, people with disabilities, and veterans make up a smaller percentage of the population, but they make up an even smaller percentage of companies. For example, women constitute 51.1 percent of the US population but only 47 percent of the total labor force.

Beyond entry-level positions, management and executive positions see the numbers of these groups shrink even more. For this reason, we will call these demographics "underrepresented groups." For stylistic reasons, this book might use terms like "marginalized communities," "minority members," and "diverse talent" as synonyms. The central term "underrepresented groups," however, foregrounds how certain kinds of thinking, perspectives, and experiences are missing from organizational decision-making because the social groups more likely to have them are more likely to be missing from those organizations.

For example, companies can do a better job of connecting with lucrative and ignored Black communities if they have team members who are from and understand those communities. Businesses trying to go global will improve their chances if they have more employees from all over the world. Organizations looking for improvisational skills, organizational flexibility, and unusual levels of resilience would improve their successes if they improved their efforts to employ military veterans.

Underrepresented groups are underutilized. Their members are overlooked, and their insights go ignored. Leaders who want to look for new ideas understand the need to search in new communities. If your team has different social identities, it increases the chances of having the different experiences that produce different perspectives. Those different perspectives yield the different thinking that generates a fuller picture, and having a fuller picture leads to the innovation that improves productivity and profitability.

Diversity: Bringing together multiple social identities to promote different thinking.

As we'll see in chapters to come, organizations thrive when they move beyond homogeneity and embrace difference. Organizations can think more creatively, plan more accurately, and consider more thoroughly when they incorporate a wide range of perspectives. Companies that seek greater diversity are on the right track, recognizing the benefits that can come from heterogeneity, but as we'll see, problems arise when diversity becomes the only goal.

Equity: The procedures that use proportionality to cultivate growth.

If diversity is the objective, equity is the structure that makes it possible. Many organizations that value diversity take a passive approach. They remove a handful of obstacles and expect change to come. In doing so, they overestimate the likelihood that people will overcome centuries of biases, social impediments, and the threat of violence to make diversity magically happen.

On the other hand, equitable leaders realize that to overcome the structures that keep organizations homogeneous, they need to develop formal plans, policies, and practices that foster heterogeneity. They don't assume people in charge of hiring, management, and promotions will just "do the right thing," nor do they trust the well intentioned to defy the status quo that surrounds them. Instead, equity creates external systems of accountability to ensure fairness can happen in the first place. Imagine diversity is like any other goal. Willpower isn't enough. Structure is what yields success.

If you want to run a marathon, determination has its place. More valuable is buying running equipment, joining a running group, and collecting donation pledges from friends. Equity is the same way. It recognizes that if diversity is your goal, you must create external structures that encourage progress toward that aim even when resolve fails, forgetfulness abounds, and you just plain old feel like sleeping in.

If diversity is the goal, equity refers to the operations that push organizations toward it.

. . .

Inclusion: Sharing authority so underrepresented groups have influence.

Beyond diversity and equity, the highest goal of DEI is inclusion. Diversity passively removes structures that keep underrepresented people out, and equity actively produces structures that ensure they can enter in, but inclusion creates opportunities for them to move up.

Diverse organizations might issue public statements, post social media messaging, and even ensure each job ad has a statement about EEOC but still fail to hire people from underrepresented groups.

Equitable companies may do the recruiting and hiring that onboards underrepresented people long enough to retain them for more than three months but still fall short when it comes to letting them advance within the organization or even get their ideas to survive up the chain long enough to make any kind of impact.

Inclusive leaders? They go further. They go beyond hiring people from underrepresented groups just to show how progressive the organization is. They go beyond recruiting marginalized people into a company only to push them to the fringes of that entity, appearing in all the publicity photos but shut out from all the meetings. Authentic allies go beyond leading organizations that include underrepresented people and give those people opportunities to reshape the policies, structures, and actions of the organization. By sharing authority, they open the door, make a path to the table, provide opportunities to speak, and actually change according to what they hear.

The organizations that are most successful are those that incorporate diversity, equity, and inclusion. They value diversity enough to remove obstacles that keep people from underrepresented groups away. They go further, however, and pursue diversity through equity that reinforces these pursuits on a procedural level. Ultimately, they strive for a greater goal of inclusivity, where structures exist that ensure people from underrepresented groups have the ability to change the organization.

Working with these definitions and concepts, *Actions Speak Louder* shows readers how to achieve diversity, equity, and inclusion in ways that benefit everyone.

Looking toward the Future

Since June 2020, DEI-related job openings have risen by 55 percent. Beyond this change in market demand, there has been a cultural shift in what prospective employees expect. For example, people increasingly want organizations to take a stand on racial justice, and employees are expecting employers to take actionable steps toward greater inclusion. In the end, this market demand and cultural shift show the ways in which DEI has become a business imperative.

Increasingly, that vital practice relies on direct managers. Frances Brooks Taplett, Jennifer Garcia-Alonso, Matt Krentz, and Mai-Britt Poulsen are consultants with the Boston Consulting Group. They note that senior executives, board members, major investors, and employees want DEI. In this context, companies value leaders who can diversify business thinking, turn privilege into potential, and make the moral and business case for inclusion. More than ever, DEI is becoming a skill that helps leaders gain competency, engage their employees, and advance in their field. The leaders who are prepared for the twenty-first century are ready for this reality. In addition to business communication, managerial economics, and supply-chain management, they are competent in discussions about bias, privilege, and microaggressions. Instead of just handing this work off to HR or the DEI task force, they participate in an organization's inclusivity initiatives. In short, the leaders of the future are those who recognize DEI as a leadership value. Whether you've been doing this work for years or are just starting your journey, the fact that you've begun reading this book at all shows that you also recognize this value.

Despite the horrific past of business in the United States, *Actions Speak Louder* hopes for a better future, one full of both physical and psychological safety where people from all backgrounds can thrive without fear and advance without terror. It strives to create a world that Uncle Buck never got to enjoy. Innumerable people have toiled through difficulties to become historical "firsts" in their fields and ensured they wouldn't be the last. Indebted to them, this book offers tools that will help leaders create a more inclusive world.

The only thing matched by the hopes I have for this book is the expectations I have for its readers. Many communities have lived in the shadows of stories like those of Uncle Buck. Countless tales are passed between family members regarding injustices that befell those from underrepresented backgrounds who dared to strive for life, liberty, and the pursuit of happiness. For centuries, those stories have been ignored, dismissed, and denied.

But the summer of 2020 felt different. With a swiftness, width, and depth I'd never seen, voices came out in support of African Americans. In the same week George Floyd was murdered, celebrities, politicians, and CEOs declared that Black lives matter. What's more, they made public commitments to improve the lives of Black people. Inspired by the outpouring of support and the reckoning Americans have made, I am filled with a new hope. But more excited than hearing these declarations, I am excited to witness their deeds. Why? Because we all know, that despite the value and volume of words, actions speak louder.

PART I

Personal
Development

CHAPTER ONE

Use Your Privilege
Identifying Your Workplace
Privileges

From the Block to the Boardroom

Spending years behind desks, staring at screens, and doing work so removed from immediate impact, I revere people who walk the streets and meet the people where they are: the elder who spends retirement running a community garden that employs kids from low-income neighborhoods, the peer who goes to murder scenes and prevents retaliation, and full-time doulas who spend long hours in maternity wards to improve birth outcomes for underserved populations.

This drive to get back among the people almost drove me to leave a job as the CEO of a multimillion-dollar foundation. The position was fulfilling, and it gave me the opportunity to fund amazing work. But I wanted to move beyond supporting the people who worked on the front lines, so I could have more direct impact.

During this time, I attended a conference for Black foundation leaders. There, I met many like me, professionals who worked to serve the underprivileged and felt ambivalent about being so far removed from them.

On the final night of the conference, a colleague recalled a story where she sat in her high-rise office looking down on the streets below as they filled with marching protestors. Seeing the dedication of the crowds, she felt a pang of guilt. It grilled her, asking, "Who do you think you are? Better than them? Sellout sitting up here while your people are struggling down there. If you really cared, you'd go down there with them."

Unable to bear another minute of this interrogation, she changed her shoes, stormed out of her office, and hit the elevator button. As she descended, her thoughts began to race. Not only would she join the march that night, she'd join again the next day. She'd join the movement, dedicate herself to the cause, and quit her job.

When she stepped out the front door of her building and onto the street, she saw a pastor from the neighborhood. She ran to him and said she was ready. She looked for a picket sign and listened for the chants to repeat before rattling off her plans—this march, the one tomorrow, and then quitting on Friday so she could give her full attention to the cause.

But that was when the smiling reverend scoffed that she didn't have to be so extreme. She could march tonight, work tomorrow, and march the next night. She didn't have to quit one to do the other. He told her to look at all the people marching, a whole line of people filling the street. There were plenty of people who could march, but few had her privileges. According to him, the organizers needed her to be in that office representing them when nobody else would. They would be on the block, but they also needed her in the boardroom.

Having the education that can gain a job, the social stability to retain a career, and the resources to read this book is a privilege. Sometimes that advantage can seem like a disgrace that makes some want to quit so they can join the march down on the block forever. At the same time, however, that privilege can also provide opportunities to achieve goals even up in the boardroom. People in our position have privilege. Facing that reality, many feel the shame that compels them to deny its existence, and others experience the guilt that drives them to renounce it.

But advantages can become ethical if you use them to benefit the disadvantaged. For this reason, this chapter will walk the fine line of avoiding the temptation to either deny privilege or renounce it. Later chapters will explore organizational changes at the level of practices, policies, and operations, but to increase the likelihood that those other goals will succeed, start with identifying ways to use your privilege.

Defining Workplace Privileges

The most popular text regarding privilege is "White Privilege: Unpacking the Invisible Knapsack." In that article, Peggy McIntosh, former associate director of the Wellesley Centers for Women, focuses on the racial advantages whiteness affords people in the United States. Some examples she covers include the following: "If I should need to move, I can be pretty sure of renting or purchasing housing in an area which I can afford and in which I want to live"; I can be pretty sure that my neighbors in such a location will be neutral or pleasant to me"; "I can go shopping alone most of the time, pretty well assured that I will not be followed or harassed"; I can turn on the television or open to the front page of the paper and see people of my race widely represented"; "When I am told about our national heritage or about 'civilization,' I am shown that people of my color made it what it is."

Over time, the concept of privilege has taken on a life of its own in public discourse. Some assume that claiming someone has privilege suggests they've had no difficulties at all. Some argue that the phrase "White privilege" implies every White person is racist, oppresses people of color, and enjoys the rewards of a racially unequal society.

For our purposes here, privilege has a different meaning. Here, privilege means gaining benefits based on your social identity. Everyone has certain privileges in certain situations. For example, I am a woman of color, and the meaning of that identity differs from one context to the next. In certain spaces, my racial identity presents challenges, but in other places, my education, work experience, and financial security grant me opportunities. While I might not have racial privilege in relationship to White people, having lighter skin means I have it in comparison to darker people. I am a woman who doesn't have the social privileges attached to being a man, but being cisgender shields me from the particular social disadvantages reserved for transgender people.

In addition to recognizing the degree to which everyone has certain privileges, it is important to remember the level to which everyone has certain difficulties. A White woman might have racial privilege but not gender privilege. A Black man might have gender privilege but not racial privilege. There are White business managers struggling to pay back student loans, make the mortgage, and save for retirement, all while knowing they are two checks away from financial ruin. Reductive definitions of White privilege can suggest that the 15.9 million White people who live below the poverty line in the United States have access to unbelievable riches when so many make less than $25,000 a year.

For these reasons, when talking about "privilege," this chapter won't imply that the people who have things like native-born, Christian, or neurotypical social identities automatically live a life of ease. Furthermore, having any kind of privilege doesn't mean someone intentionally stole advantages from another or consciously participates in immoral actions that ensure others suffer disadvantages. Certain social contexts privilege certain social identities. Regardless of who we are, what we think, or what we do, just showing up in particular social contexts with specific social identities gives us certain kinds of privileges.

While widening out privilege to address multiple kinds, it is also important to narrow our scope. When people talk about privileges, they usually concentrate on a broad kind. Most focus on social, political, legal, psychological, and cultural privileges. In these aspects, to have privilege means my group's values structure social interactions; my group is overrepresented in politics; my group's interests drive the creation and enforcement of laws; my group enjoys psychological comfort, security, and confidence; and my group membership grants me the cultural benefits that come from being overrepresented in media.

Besides social, political, legal, psychological, and cultural privileges that garner the most attention in conversations about privilege, there are also workplace privileges. We will define workplace privileges as gaining workplace benefits based on your social identity. Social privilege decides who's more likely to survive an encounter with police. Political privilege dictates who won't have to prove their humanity in front of the Supreme Court. Legal privilege determines who will get released on bail, found guilty, or sentenced longer. In light of these big issues, workplace privileges can seem relatively insignificant, but they are important. The gateway to social, political, legal, psychological, and cultural advantages is economic power. Ultimately, if they are the key to the economic power, workplace privileges become the nexus for others.

Identifying Your Workplace Privileges

Now that we've defined workplace privileges, we're going to do what I call creating a "Dinner Table."

Over the next few pages, this Dinner Table exercise will help you identify your own workplace privileges. I understand this process can be uncomfortable, but please gather the courage to examine yourself. This process isn't designed to inspire moral guilt. Trust me that we will end this chapter by turning it into a constructive exercise that will benefit others. But before we get to thinking about how you can "use your privilege," you must first take an honest inventory of what your privileges are. In private, with nothing but the truth and your conscience, please take a few moments to circle the following workplace privileges that apply to you, in the Porcelain column of the below chart.

DINNER TABLE

Porcelain	Thali
1. I can assume coworkers won't ignore me because of my social identity.	
2. I can presume that if I get loud, animated, or even angry in a meeting and ask challenging questions, my social identity will help me seem rational and assertive as opposed to emotional and aggressive.	
3. I can presuppose that the neighborhood surrounding my workplace, access to the building, and spaces within it won't pose a threat to me.	
4. I can feel included in office culture, surrounded by people I feel comfortable with and who feel comfortable with me.	

5. I take it for granted that most office policies, rules, and codes of conduct already conform to the norms of my social identity group, and I don't have to change anything about what I already do in order to automatically comply with them.

6. I don't have to work extraordinarily hard to ensure my ideas are heard in meetings, elevated during discussions, and advanced beyond conversations to travel up to levels where decisions are made.

7. I can expect social functions essential to networking and my professional advancement to involve activities that conform to the values of my social group.

8. I've never thought I'd be asked to do extra, unpaid work (lead employee resource groups [ERGs], create affinity groups, hold learning sessions, conduct town halls, or start mentorships) related to my social group.

9. I can assume all my options for self-identification appear on the official forms my workplace uses.	
10. I have a social position that grants me and employers the ability to reasonably predict my job performance.	
11. I've never felt the pressure of representing my entire social identity group.	
12. I have transportation accessibility that makes commuting easy.	
13. I understand the cultural references that dominate workplace conversation.	
14. I can relate to small talk about hobbies, weekend activities, and cultural events.	
15. I can avoid people from social identity groups I've been taught to mistrust.	

16. I'm confident people won't avoid me or fail to invite me to social activities because of my social identity.	
17. People won't make assumptions about my professionalism based on my name.	
18. Most organizational leaders are from my social group.	
19. I work in a place where most people are from my social group.	
20. I won't be expected to be a representative expert on the history, psychology, culture, sociology, and politics of my social group.	
21. I won't feel alienated, threatened, or endangered by the dominant group in response to events on the news concerning my social group.	
22. People won't misidentify my role, position, or title in the organization.	

23. I won't feel the pressure to overperform so I can positively represent my entire social group.	
24. Organizational policies are made with my social group in mind.	
25. Standards of professionalism reflect the values of my social group.	
26. I am more likely to be perceived as competent and professional even if I'm not.	
27. I can use public facilities without fear of verbal abuse, psychological intimidation, physical violence, or arrest.	
28. I don't have to worry about being misgendered or misnamed.	
29. My mental and physical ability and behavior will conform with the criteria assumed to indicate "good work" and "high engagement."	

30. My office will be closed on religious holidays that conform to my belief system.	
31. Because of my age, people assume I am more competent.	
32. I can feel comfortable inviting my partner to work events.	
33. I can lift the weight often required as a prerequisite for many jobs.	
34. I can assume my language (vocabulary, grammar, accent, volume, speech patterns, cultural references, diction level) will improve instead of undermine people's assumptions about my competence.	
35. I can feel confident that my military status will ensure the continuity of employment and cultural understanding others have of me that is essential to retaining a job.	

Now that you've looked at some of the most common workplace privileges, spend some time looking for others. Close your eyes and imagine an average workday from the time you leave your front door to when you walk back through it. Dig deep, pay attention to the smallest details, and ask the following:

1. Consider the environment where you work. Take into account everything from regional location in relationship to the city, physical layout from the parking lot to the building, and structure within the facility. Explore everything from the width of the hallways to the seating design in conference rooms to the artwork on the walls to the music playing in the lobby. For which social groups were these environments created?

2. Examine the practices of your workplace culture. Which social groups do they centralize? Which do they marginalize?

3. How would your normal workday differ if you were from a different social group?

4. What things that you take for granted would change?

Once you've surveyed some of the most common workplace privileges and spent a few minutes reexamining your everyday routine, take some time for reflection. Strive to be as creative and specific as possible about the everyday, common, and subtle advantages of your professional life. At the bottom of the Porcelain column, **add all the other answers that you just thought up.**

When I've done this exercise with people, many report how difficult it is. One reason for this difficulty is cultural context. In the

United States, many place a premium on self-determination. One reason why many immigrants came to the American colonies was that they wanted to decide their own career path in ways other countries wouldn't let them. The United States is a nation that was born with a Declaration of *Independence*. Followed by this revolutionary fervor was a period of transcendentalism where Emerson's "Self-Reliance" became gospel and Thoreau's *Walden* extolled individualism as a virtue. Americans are a people who popularize the phrase "pull yourself up by the bootstraps," revere the Horatio Alger type, venerate rags-to-riches stories, make a creed of the American dream, canonize "self-made billionaires," and anathematize "handouts." Sixty-five percent of American adults identify as Christian, and among that demographic, the most widely known Bible verse is "God helps those who help themselves," which doesn't even appear in the Bible. In a culture that idolizes merit, privilege becomes a cardinal sin that inspires severe guilt, dread, and repression.

Some critics believe DEI is unnecessary because they claim privilege doesn't exist or create unfair advantages. At the same time, many proponents of DEI undermine their own efforts because they fail to recognize the privileges afforded them. For example, I've seen plenty of attempts at greater inclusion disrupted by White managers who claim creating a Black ERG is unnecessary, but I've also seen plenty of disruption happen because of allies who've considered themselves honorary members of the Black ERG. The one falsely insists that there is no difference between the experiences of White and Black employees. The other admits there is a disparity between these experiences but fails to see how they have advantages their underrepresented counterparts do not.

The leaders who foster greater belonging are those who recognize unfairness but are also honest about how they benefit from it. For example, the best male mentors recognize that the assertiveness they display in meetings might prove disastrous for their female protégés. In their attempts to be allies, they remember that they receive privileges others do not. In order to craft DEI initiatives that benefit underrepresented groups, you must first recognize the advantages that the workplace affords to people from your social identity. In short, creating a more inclusive workplace for the underprivileged demands that you first recognize your privileges.

Privilege as Porcelain

Imagine privilege as dinnerware. Some have a porcelain set that is expensive, valuable, and delicate. They imagine privilege is an investment they must protect. They ignore the fact that they inherited it from people and only received it because of how they were born. Of course, they might have done a lot of work to maintain it, spent countless hours wrapping, polishing, and dusting it, but that fact doesn't mean they did anything to initially earn it.

Over time, privilege deniers might see the porcelain set as something that they deserve to own and others do not. They may install protective glass displays, video monitoring, and security systems to ensure no one accesses it. They might manipulate markets in hopes that others can't buy it, and petition the manufacturers to discontinue production, knowing that the porcelain set will increase in value only to the extent that others don't have access to it.

They will be terrified that serving food on this porcelain will devalue their property. Working so hard to safeguard their possession, they are less likely to invite visitors inside for a meal. Even offering a morsel of bread on paper plates fills them with fear that, by gaining access to the dining room, a guest might notice the porcelain set in the display case. Protecting their investment, these porcelain owners will deny they own any dinnerware at all and refuse to share even the crumbs that fall from their table, sending guests from their house still hungry.

Others—critiquers—might recognize that the porcelain set they have was handed down to them for reasons decided before they were even born. They might critique themselves and declare this inheritance unfair. They might even throw open the front door of their house and declare to all the world how much they know they got their dinnerware unjustly. They can take advantage of every opportunity to tell passersby that others are denied porcelain sets unmercifully. They may take to social media to make these proclamations, but acknowledging the fact that they unfairly possess a porcelain set does only so much good.

One night, sick of mere talk, they might go beyond critiquing their privilege to renounce it. In solidarity with those who don't have a plate to their name, they might open the protective glass case, unwrap the set, and hurl it across the room, smashing their inheritance into a thousand pieces as an act of cathartic protest.

While the actions of deniers, critiquers, and renouncers differ, their impact is similar. Even if they think their porcelain set is shameful and stomp it beyond recognition, the ends are the same for those who knock on their door with growling stomachs. Whether they insist they have no porcelain or renounce their set by smashing it into a fine powder, they turn others away.

But there are those who do something more. Instead of devoting their time, energy, and attention to porcelain, they use thali.

Privilege as Thali

Thali is something I ate off throughout my entire childhood. Every night, we'd gather around these round metal plates and feast. No one was afraid the stainless steel would dent. No one worried these rugged dishes would stain. Why? Everyone knew this type of dinnerware was made to stack, ship, and carry all kinds of food. There's no need to hide them, because they're relatively economical. No need to wrap them, because they don't scratch easily. Porcelain is an expensive and delicate investment meant to be protected, but thali is a cost-effective, tough product designed to be used. The one has worth insofar as it remains useless and brings the owner value, but the other has worth only if it becomes useful and brings value to others.

To use your privilege as thali is to use your privilege in ways that achieve fairness: set out thalis you feel no need to protect, deploy stainless steel plates you never thought were yours, and start thinking of privilege as something that was always meant to be used to benefit others, a thing given to you so that you might give.

So rather than thinking about workplace privileges as something to deny, critique, or renounce, use them in ways that benefit everyone. To practice this, rethink of privileges as opportunities. Instead of insisting you don't have privileges, simply analyzing them, or planning to quit so you can be free of them, practice a little creativity. Use the powers of problem solving to devise ways to turn those advantages into things that place you in unique positions to elevate others.

To do this, return to the Dinner Table exercise. Note all the workplace privileges you circled in the Porcelain column. Now flip them so they can become actionable items that achieve greater inclusivity in the Thali column. For each item you write in the Thali column, it's helpful to start with the prompt "Use my privilege . . . to . . ." To get you started, here are a few examples.

Porcelain	Thali
I can assume coworkers won't ignore me because of my social identity.	Use my privilege as a welcomed person to involve people from less-welcomed social identity groups, inviting them to social functions, centering their opinion during meetings, and asking them to join others for lunch.

Now that we've started the process, complete the rest of the list of other privileges generated in this chapter. Do the same with those you added on your own. Take each workplace privilege and flip it into an opportunity to use your privilege to benefit others.

One of the Most Powerful Privileges

When I conduct this Dinner Table exercise with people, many pose problems. When coming up with items for the Thali column, they cite their lack of authority, resources, or time, insisting that they don't have the power to make sweeping changes at their organization. In response, I point out that one of the most powerful privileges is being seen as objective.

You might be the CEO of your company or an entry-level team member. You could have millions for DEI initiatives or no budget at all. Maybe you're the DEI officer whose sole responsibility is creating inclusivity, or you're an exhausted worker volunteering your time to improve the workplace. Regardless of your position, there are opportunities to use the privilege of seeming politically neutral. Americans are more likely to assume people who are straight, White, cisgender, non-disabled, or male are "rational." For this reason, when a person who occupies any of these social identities does something as simple as agree with the ideas of another who does not, they can impart the aura of "rationality" upon ideas that would otherwise be dismissed as the political agenda of a jaded minority.

Even if you don't belong to all the social groups that are seen as rational, simply belonging to a social group other than the one for which you're advocating can achieve the persuasive power that comes from seeming more objective. Business professors Denise Lewin Loyd and Lisa M. Amoroso note that American workers are more likely to be suspicious of intra-identity advocacy. For example, when women advocate for "women's issues" or Black people push for reforms that benefit them, others tend to dismiss these efforts as self-ishly motivated and, therefore, invalid.

In this situation, advocacy across social identities is important. Studies show that inter-identity advocacy can be more effective re-gardless of the particular identities of the advocates. Even people from underrepresented groups can be taken more seriously if they espouse policies that benefit communities to which they don't belong. For example, calls for gender-neutral bathrooms are more likely to be taken as logical if supported by cisgender and gender-conforming people. Requests for more universally accessible buildings will gain more traction if backed by non-disabled people.

Many dismiss even the most modest requests to improve work-places in ways that might benefit social identity groups as self-serving impositions. To sidestep this assumption, be sure to also bolster causes for inclusion that don't benefit your social group. You may identify as a member of a minority community, but you still have privilege you can use to benefit others. Cishet women can advocate for LGBTQ+ issues. Non-disabled Black people can strive for greater accessibility.

At the same time, avoid falling into the trap of saviorism. It is one thing to identify your privileges, but it is quite another to identify how you should best use them to benefit others. Underrepresented groups aren't helpless, and they don't need you to save them. As the beneficiary of certain privileges, you are positioned to support initia-tives they lead, but make sure you find ways to take a back seat, stay out of the way, amplify, and follow.

Allyship, by definition, means supporting communities other than your own. Regardless of your rank, title, or position within your organization, find creative ways to identify the privileges you do have. Despite the standing, power, and position of your group within society, seek out ways you can advocate for others. Before jumping to the sweeping, long-term, and widespread changes you want to make so your entire organization becomes more inclusive, start with the immediate, short-term, and particular workplace advantages you enjoy every day. Start by setting the Dinner Table. Understand Porcelain columns. Create Thali ones.

CHAPTER TWO

Check Yourself
Diversifying Your Business Thinking

Take out a piece of paper. At the top, title it "Green Rabbits Graph." Beneath this title, draw three columns. For now, skip the first column and go to the second. Title it "Unprofessionalism." In a moment, under that heading, you're going to list all the behaviors and characteristics you'd list as unprofessional. Don't include things that break the law or violate organizational codes of conduct or employee handbooks in ways that should result in obvious termination. Focus on those that are too ambiguous to appear in these legal documents but remain so obviously wrong to you that they appear on your list of nonnegotiables.

If it helps, think of a coworker that you think is excruciatingly unprofessional. Be specific. What are the concrete, empirical things they do that lead you to give them this label? Think about particular criteria: clothing, hair, jewelry, makeup, posture, speech volume, speech speed, laughter (at all, not at all, frequency, timing, volume), storytelling, vocabulary, idioms, references, facial expressions, lack of facial expressions, gestures, use of space, office space decorations, car, bumper stickers, walking speed, formality with written communication (salutations, grammar, sign-offs, etc.) type of written communication (email, text, business communication platform, etc.), and pleasantries.

Go deeper and interrogate that deepest reservoir of uninterrogated assumptions: manners. What behaviors do you think are unequivocally rude, impolite, or disrespectful? (Again, do not include illegal, fireable, or clear violations.) Use this information to do the following: **List all the things that are obviously "unprofessional."**

Professional Biases

In "Top 10 Reasons for Getting Fired," career expert Alison Doyle compiles some of the most common justifications for termination. They include calling in sick with a fake excuse, being late, and disrupting other employees. For many, these seem like universal standards of professionalism, but they are also the relative standards constructed by particular social groups that favor their living conditions and perceptions. Calling in sick with a "fake" excuse might seem like an objective reason to fire someone, but it is also a reason that is biased against women who are more likely to have to call in sick the next time their child is off school.

"Being late" might seem like a uniform excuse for termination, but it could also be biased against, for example, a Puerto Rican employee who is late because they come from a culture that values multigenerational living and they were taking care of an elderly relative.

"Disrupting other employees" seems like a clear waste of resources that warrants dismissal, but what if the "disruptive" team member is from Thailand and spends time forging interpersonal connections?

In these situations, biases against these employees can get them fired, and in turn, organizations can end up harming themselves. The woman who has to call in sick with a "fake" excuse to stay with her child can be more productive than the men who are more "honest." If instead of firing her, employers gave her flexible scheduling, a time-strapped mother might complete more work from home between the hours of five and nine than the counterparts who have perfect attendance but might spend much of their nine-to-five looking like they're working.

If the Puerto Rican worker had permission to arrive late so they could care for a loved one, they could experience the improved morale that would increase their productivity beyond that of punctual employees.

The Thai worker who "wasted" a few minutes every day talking to coworkers could improve long-term retention even among the American-born workers who are so focused on spending time wisely and not disrupting others that they end up lonely enough to quit. In the long run, the "disruptive" worker could save the company untold fortunes in turnover costs and make the organization more money than those who never disrupt their coworkers until they unexpectedly leave a job vacancy that disrupts those workers for months to come.

In these instances, these actions seem like universal reasons to terminate employment. It seems like common sense that calling in is dishonest, tardiness is disrespectful, and disruptions are rude. Armed with moralistic terms like "deceit," "contempt," and "discourtesy," a leader might feel justified firing these people. The underlying business justification is that liars, insubordinates, and brutes undermine the productivity, profitability, and retention that is essential to running a company. However, as we've seen in these examples, these supposedly universal standards that take on moral significance actually betray biases in favor of certain groups.

If you fire the woman because calling in undermines productivity, but she actually increases productivity, are you firing her for business reasons or for biased ones that disproportionately punish women and protect men? If you terminate the late employee because tardiness compromises profitability, but that employee actually improves profitability, are you grounding that termination in business reasons or in biases that favor workers who conform to the Eurocentric practice of living in single-family homes and putting elderly relatives in assisted living facilities? If you dismiss the Thai worker for disrupting others because disruption causes turnover, but that worker's "disruption" actually improves retention, does your dismissal stem from responsible business leadership or from irresponsible biases that privilege American work styles that are renowned for being cold and impersonal?

Is It Really about the Individual?

While the previous section focused on how the standards of "professionalism" can be culturally relative, the fact remains that even the standards that seem most universally objective are unequally enforced. In "Black Workers Really Do Need to Be Twice as Good," Gillian B. White shows the many ways Black workers are overscrutinized and under-rewarded even when they have the same performance as their White counterparts. Economists Costa Cavounidis and Kevin Lang find that Black workers are more likely to be fired for offenses than White employees who commit the same offenses. They are also less likely to receive promotions or raises for achieving the same accomplishments as their White counterparts.

People who scrutinize and reward in racially biased ways insist they aren't bigoted. Most insist the racial identity of an employee has nothing to do with the reasons why they report, reprimand, warn, or fire someone. But when they deny the role bias can play in thinking, they deceive themselves. In *Sway: Unravelling Unconscious Bias*, Pragya Agarwal notes that while many might not recognize their unconscious bigotry, people in this kind of denial still experience cognitive dissonance. She notes that in cultures that discourage bias, this cognitive dissonance masks itself from the person who feels it. Instead of admitting bias against an entire *racial* group, they will insist they are acting against an *individual* person's actions, attitude, manners, personality, or character.

In the workplace, these general attitudes all tie into assumptions about what it means to be "professional." Despite the statistics that show disparities in firing are rooted in racial identity, people who do this firing insist they monitor, reprimand, and terminate those who are "unprofessional." Many grounds for separation concentrate on specific incidents, a particular infraction or a period of underperformance, some concrete action where someone did something wrong or failed to do something right, a straw that broke the camel's back. But supervisors are more likely to find these specific moments that could justify firing based on innumerable indistinct moments that could not. Research by White, Cavounidis, Lang, and Agarwal shows that, while workers from both minority and majority groups commit fireable offenses, supervisors are more likely to notice those committed by people from underrepresented groups. According to the saying, "if a cop follows you for 500 miles, you're going to get a ticket." The issue is that rule enforcers don't follow everyone equally. As the research shows, supervisors are more likely to micromanage people from underrepresented groups. That micromanagement increases the likelihood of finding "unprofessionalism," not because marginalized groups are more unprofessional but because managers are less likely to monitor their overrepresented counterparts.

Vague Impressions

Labeling someone as "unprofessional" is informed by countless impressions that seem to have nothing to do with social identity. To see how this is the case, look back at the list you wrote at the beginning of this chapter. How many of the things you wrote under the "Unprofessionalism" column disproportionately apply to an underrepresented social group? Chances are a fair number of them. Why? Because people are socialized to confuse the relative values of some with universal truths for all.

For example, the definition of professional clothing favors the style valued by certain ethnic groups, cultures, and socioeconomic classes, and it deems all others "unprofessional." Standards of what constitutes professional, appropriate, and "groomed" hair disproportionately punishes Black styles like Afros, braids, and locs. Some even border on requiring people with naturally curly hair to chemically straighten it.

If a Black woman wears bright colors, locs, big earrings, and no makeup, she's more likely to be seen as "a little rough around the edges" before she even takes her seat during her first day of work. If she squints her eyes .35 millimeters more, speaks .67 decibels louder, and talks 7.3 words per minute faster than the undefined average of her White male supervisors, she can appear unpolished before the end of her first meeting. If she laughs .7 seconds longer than, tells stories 1.7 times more frequently than, and has a vocabulary that varies by 19.7 percent from those of her leaders, she can seem to be misaligned with the company's culture by the end of the week.

Of course, these measurements would be near impossible to come by. In fact, it seems humorous to even give them this degree of specificity. Nevertheless, there is a line. That line might be unconscious. But there is a line between the kinds of idioms, references, and facial expressions you can use and those you cannot. There is a line between the kinds of gestures, use of space, and cubicle decorations that will improve managerial perceptions of you and those that will not. There is a line between the kinds of cars to drive, salutations to give, and pleasantries to recite that will make you seem to have the "right" comportment and those that will not.

In short, while they might be too constant to be imperceptible and too innumerable to be empirical, these characteristics carry infinite weight when it comes to who gets reprimanded or rewarded, punished or praised, fired or promoted. Of course, no leader with even a basic understanding of employment law would fire somebody for their walking speed, but the pace of one's stride can be the thing that becomes the unconscious and ridiculous warrant that authorizes the investigation that finds justification for termination later. In short, the fundamental and unavoidable issue that remains even for the most inclusive leaders is the need to confront our professional biases.

Cui Bono?

In my work as an attorney, I loved the phrase "Cui bono?," which translates as "who benefits?" When evaluating a policy, it's important to investigate how it came to be. Instead of assuming it came down from the heavens as an eternal virtue, it's important to ask, "Who benefits?" from a particular rule.

Return to your Green Rabbits Graph. Look at what you wrote under the Unprofessionalism column, and ask, "Cui bono?"

If you're like any number of participants we've had do similar exercises, you probably have very strong reasons for listing these characteristics in this column. At the same time, I'd humbly ask you to revisit some of them. Oftentimes, respondents have characteristics of unprofessionalism that include being "uncivil," "disrespectful," or "ignorant." While civility, respect, and knowledge seem like non-negotiable qualities every good employee must have, the situation is a little more complicated.

"Civility" tends to serve the status quo. It concentrates on obeying rules that have been constructed by those who created the status quo and continue to benefit from it. Charges of incivility can be used to police Black women who are more direct than leaders would like. "Respect" tends to focus on culturally specific ideals of what respect means. Therefore, a worker from the Netherlands might give direct negative feedback in ways an American worker might think is disrespectful. But that Dutch employee might think they were paying the highest respect by avoiding the diplomatic qualifiers common in American discourse and aim for brutal honesty. Discussing "knowledge" fails to specify which knowledge. It suggests a person is either professionally knowledgeable or not without appreciating the extent to which everyone has a particular kind of knowledge that might affect them negatively in some professional contexts but can prove beneficial in others. For example, people on the autism spectrum can display a wide range of neurodiversity that makes it hard for them to understand some things that people could take for granted while simultaneously making other connections that neurotypical people do not.

So return to your Green Rabbits Graph, and ask, "Cui bono?" In the first column, write "Bias." Note each characteristic listed in the Unprofessionalism column. In the Bias column, write the social group that most benefits from that criterion of professionalism. For example, if you listed "laughing too loudly" as a characteristic of unprofessionalism, ethnic groups that are more likely to laugh quietly or not at all are more likely to benefit from that criterion. If you wrote "respect," American notions of what respectful looks like would inordinately benefit Americans. **Take a moment and go through the first column, noting which social group is privileged by each characteristic of "unprofessionalism,"** like this:

Bias	Unprofessionalism
Cultures that value quieter laughing	Laughing too loudly

In a little while, we'll finish the third and final column. But before we do that, a few words about diversifying our thinking.

Diversifying Your Thinking

If bias informs how we perceive the performance of our coworkers, we've got some work to do. Implementing policies and making public statements are important for creating an inclusive workplace, but how do we create greater inclusivity in our own minds? We can create organizational systems to prevent others from obviously discriminating against people when it comes to hiring, firing, promoting, and awarding bonuses, but we must also develop individual processes to prevent ourselves from subtly fostering the biased judgments that lead to these inequitable forms of punishment. How we perceive the professionalism of others can be so insidious because it can inform our judgments of coworkers even more than the blatant criteria we use to decide whom to reward and whom to punish. To make more accurate, fair, and productive decisions, we must counter biases.

There are a few ways to do this. The first concentrates on examining the problem, exploring how pervasive and problematic biases are. For example, you just filled out the left column of your table, seeing how criteria of unprofessionalism that you might have assumed were universal actually benefit particular social groups. This exercise might reveal how inaccurate stereotypes are and how much they can harm people. Surveying historical facts, sociological data, and psychological studies can show participants in antibias training that unreasoned assumptions about social groups are rooted in stereotypes and undermine workplace inclusivity.

This approach can be valuable. It shows people that what they think is the truth isn't. It can help participants realize the differences between their assumptions about social groups and reality. But "anti-bias training" concentrates on combating bias. Unfortunately, examining the problems of prejudices isn't the same as practicing more inclusive decision-making.

To illustrate the limits of the "anti-" approach, please humor me during a visualization exercise. Clear your mind. Ease your tension. Pay attention to the mental images that come as you read the next sentence:

"No matter what you do, don't think of a white bear."

Okay. What did you think of? A white bear! The very thing you were told to not think about became the precise thing you thought about. No matter how much we try, we can't get rid of ideas once they're thought. That's the conclusion arrived at by social psychologist Daniel Wegner. He and his team ran an experiment where they told participants not to think of a white bear, and found that all respondents imagined the exact thing they didn't want to visualize. What's worse, the harder they tried not to think about them, the more they did.

Wegner called this phenomenon "the paradoxical effects of thought suppression." According to this concept, the more we try to suppress a thought, the more we think about it. The more we think about not biting our fingernails, the more we want to. The more we tell ourselves to ignore a side ache during a marathon, the more likely we are to end up succumbing to it. The more we try to force ourselves into not thinking biased thoughts, the more susceptible we will become to them.

But let's try another visualization exercise. Like the first time, clear your mind, ease your tension, and pay attention to the mental images that come to you as you read the next sentence:

"*Do* think of green rabbits."

You just did! Like our experiment with the white bears, you thought most about the image that came to mind. However, there is a profound difference between the two experiments. In the first, you were told *not* to think of white bears. In the second, you were told *to* think of green rabbits, and you did. But what if the goal in both cases was to not think about white bears. If you focus on trying *not* to think of something, you will. But if you focus on trying to *not* think of one thing by trying *to* think of something else, you'll succeed.

According to psychologists Paula T. Hertel and Gina Calcaterra, to counter the paradoxical effects of thought suppression, you have to utilize the benefits of thought *substitution*. Some can overcome the habit of biting their fingernails by focusing on chewing gum instead. To run through the side ache, you have to think about how great it will feel finishing the marathon.

The virtues of thought replacement apply to bias. To diversify our business thinking, we can start with the problems—the stereotypes, images, thoughts, phrases, and actions to avoid. But we must also go beyond antibias thought suppression to foster pro-inclusive thought substitution. Instead of focusing on the prejudicial assumptions to avoid, we must also concentrate on the inclusive thinking to embrace.

We can know that American businesses have a proven track record of overscrutinizing the actions of their Black employees, but that knowledge on its own won't do us much good. We can understand that definitions of professionalism are culturally biased, but that critique of traditional thinking can take us only so far. Why? Because more than abhorring unfairness, the mind abhors a vacuum.

It can resolve to avoid vices, but if it doesn't have virtues to pursue, it will backslide. The mind will return to old patterns of thinking if it doesn't know what else to do.

Bias Substitution

To practice bias substitution, go beyond simply exposing the biases that lead us to denigrating certain behaviors, and start considering the overlooked benefits of them. Replace white bears with green rabbits, and flip the script. Instead of just recognizing the problems that come from narrow definitions of "unprofessionalism," consider the benefits that can come from wider definitions of "professionalism."

StrengthsFinder 2.0 is the only book that has remained in the Amazon top ten every year for a decade and ranks as the number one worldwide business bestseller. One reason it resonates with audiences is that it concentrates on strengths. While many approaches to psychology concentrate on how to avoid damaging behaviors, positive psychology focuses on how to foster beneficial outcomes. The strengths-based approach becomes a powerful business tool because it concentrates on improving the strengths one already has rather than possibly wasting energy repairing the weaknesses one might never overcome. Organizations all over the world have practiced this method. Many leaders use it to help individual team members with professional development. If a worker fixates on their problems with strategic planning, a leader might help them build on the strengths they already have in adaptability. If another keeps getting hung up on their inability to adjust quickly, a manager might help them further develop their gifts of concentration, self-discipline, and determination.

We adopt positive psychology to individual personalities all the time, but what if we did the same with social identities? While millions can recognize the values of different personality traits, what if we saw the virtues of characteristics deemed unprofessional that are common to social groups? Instead of relying on the biases that dismiss the culturally relative behavior of underrepresented groups as unprofessional behaviors to be punished, what if we saw them as strengths to build upon?

Greg and Lakisha

Let's practice diversifying our professional thinking through this lens of positive psychology with the following example. Three months after hiring both Greg and Lakisha, you're reviewing their progress. You note that Greg has secured an enormously lucrative account in Brazil's international market. While the trips he makes there are expensive, he tries to make them as quick and economical as possible. You also see that Lakisha works hard and spends long hours in multiple meetings with the same fifteen clients, but she hasn't received formal arrangements with any of them. She also has concentrated on African American markets in her hometown that don't have the global reach you expected when asking your new hires to tap into new markets.

According to traditional standards of professionalism, Greg is outperforming his counterpart. Take a few moments to think about why.

Based on the information I provided, most will assume Greg

seems more professional because he has secured a large account and moved internationally. He makes trips but keeps them quick to save money. Now, moving beyond traditional business thinking and diversifying your business thinking, what are the strengths of Lakisha's performance? Take a few moments to write some answers.

By spending long hours in multiple meetings with a small group, she is fostering long-term relationships. By meeting with the same clients, she is cultivating sustainable performance. Meeting with fifteen of them, she's diversifying her revenue streams. Concentrating on African American markets, she is reaching a new community. Focusing on her hometown, she's tapping into a demographic of which she has particular knowledge. Fixing on a nearby area, she reduces traveling expenses. While she might not yield big short-term gains, she might usher in even bigger, more reliable gains over the long term.

In many situations, leaders rush to judgment. Assuming certain criteria are universal indicators of professionalism and business value, they fail to see the virtues of other approaches. They promote Greg only to have his one $5 million deal collapse once Brazil's economy takes a downturn, and they let Lakisha go just weeks before all fifteen of her contacts could sign the deals that could bring in $15 million. Assuming they objectively read the data, they fail to see the ways in which bias influences which data they read. The numbers might not lie, but the minds of the people reading them constantly distort the truth. To avoid undermining yourself, recognize the ways in which bias infiltrates your professional judgments. To replace bias suppression with bias substitution, practice seeing the virtues of underrepresented approaches that you'd usually ignore.

Practice

To practice this bias substitution, return to your Green Rabbits Graph. Look at the list you wrote under the heading Unprofessionalism. Cross out that title and write, "White Bears." In the third column, write a title that reads "Green Rabbits." In a moment, we'll have you go through every "unprofessional" characteristic and write its professional benefits. This might require some creativity, so budget plenty of time. It might also pose some difficulties, so here are some examples.

Let's imagine that some of your white bears were "incivility," "disrespect," and "ignorance." Bias suppression would recognize that "civility," "respect," and "ignorance" tend to favor those who define these terms in ways we already explored. But bias substitution would go further. The virtue of green rabbits would invite inclusive leaders to diversify their thinking and consider the possible business benefits of these criteria that seem so obviously unprofessional.

For example, if someone seems "uncivil," they can provide challenging, unvarnished truth. American business culture has "manners" that seem polite, but that code of conduct might just produce docility and keep people from telling authority figures the very things that would be in a leader's best interests. People from groups with "uncivil" practices can state the obvious things others are too afraid to point out, ask the questions everyone wants to ask, and expand the thinking you hire people to bring. Their bluntness could boost the courage of others, raise morale, and improve retention.

If an employee comes from a background with practices that seem "disrespectful," they might improve business. While organizations can't tolerate illegal, discriminatory, or abusive behavior that undermines productivity, they often classify as "disrespectful" plenty of behaviors that do none of these things. Most important, many leaders conflate disrespect with insubordination, and confuse questions for subversion. For example, the Dutch worker who is direct with his negative feedback about a leader's plan might embarrass the leader, but that directness could benefit the business. Comments that challenge, questions that press the powerful to justify themselves, and pushback that undermines the status quo can enrage an executive who expects conversational patterns that conform to American definitions of "respect." At the same time, those comments might be just the thing that catches a multimillion-dollar mistake. Questions that ask for reasoning could be the exact vehicle that makes leaders realize the flaws in their thinking. Resistance that seems to undermine authority could be the nudge that dismantles harmful power dynamics and ushers in more egalitarian approaches a company needs to reach the next level.

Imagine your organization employed an accountant who was on the autism spectrum and they seemed "ignorant" regarding the basic operation of your business. You might feel the need to fire them. You would insist the reason wasn't their neurodiversity but that you need everyone to have baseline information to work for the company. However, the fact that the worker was on the autism spectrum would create a situation where you would be more likely to be suspicious of their cognitive abilities and therefore more likely to notice their "ignorance" when compared with all your other employees who exhibit neurotypical behavior enough to hide how little they know about your organization. But before you fire that worker, insisting that for safety's sake everyone in the factory must know proper procedures on the manufacturing floor, ask yourself whether someone in accounting who never walks that floor, regardless of their neurotypical status, really needs to understand how a forklift works. Under the guise of safety, under the badge of "knowledge," you might fire the same accountant who might not understand some things but is weeks away from recognizing shipping methods that could save the company millions. Everyone is ignorant in some areas. Being "knowledgeable" doesn't mean a person has knowledge in all things, and not knowing some things can make one likely to know other things.

If you want to embrace new possibilities, redefine professionalism. If you want the innovative thinking that underrepresented groups have to offer, pinpoint the business criteria that have been elevated by overrepresented groups and consider the benefits of those that have been ignored.

For each characteristic written in the White Bears column, go to the Green Rabbits column and write a benefit. Take a moment to do this now. Here's an example.

Bias	~~Unprofessionalism~~ White Bears	Green Rabbits
Cultures with the power to define 'civility'	Incivility	Courage

Check Yourself

In *Erasing Institutional Bias*, DEI experts Tiffany Jana and Ashley Diaz Mejias detail how organizational biases preserve the status quo. While companies develop thinking that perpetuates norms, they also spend lots of time, money, and energy trying to foster innovation. They spend billions of dollars every year trying to garner fresh perspectives. However, the very things you think are unprofessional might be the precise sources of low-cost creativity you've been looking for. Practice bias substitution by noting all the behaviors you have professional biases against. Check yourself. Be honest about all the things you think are just plain old "stupid, rude, backward, ghetto, tacky, gauche, girly, flamboyant, butch, ridiculous, naive, impractical, overly idealistic, a little much, over the top," or all the other words people use for shortcuts to dismiss something without interrogating their assumptions about it.

These are your white bears. Instead of relying on your determination to just will them away, replace them with green rabbits. Engage in the difficult, scalp-tingling, and terribly frustrating creative process of finding virtues even in, and especially in, the culturally relative behaviors you think are the most obviously unprofessional.

No one is objective. Everyone has biases. Your judgments of other people's professionalism aren't as empirical as you'd like to believe. You might research all the statistics, reports, and data when it comes time to make big decisions like who gets hired, fired, reprimanded, and promoted. But that finite number of stats, reports, and data is informed and even overwhelmed by the innumerable moments of informal research when you made assessments about subordinates, peers, or superiors based on things like the length of a skirt, the thickness of an accent, or the smell of a lunch that just came out of the microwave.

The point isn't to believe you could ever stop yourself from making unconscious judgments about someone once you've determined their attire is too revealing, their r's roll too long, or their curry smells too strong. Instead, the point is to evoke positive psychology, use bias substitution, and make conscious efforts to remember that the criteria of professionalism we assume is universal is particular to specific social groups. Find virtues in the values of the behaviors that underrepresented people bring to the organization. Substitute your biases. Complete your Green Rabbits Graph. To diversify your business thinking, find the professional benefits that can come only from green rabbits. In short, check yourself.

CHAPTER THREE

Build a Bridge
Making the Case for DEI

After millions saw footage of George Floyd being murdered, people realized the United States must review its law enforcement policies. The country must interrogate the practices whereby an unarmed person can be killed by police officers. At the same time, when I think about the arrest on May 25, 2020, that ended Floyd's life, I can't help but remember that these tragic events all happened because police were called over an allegedly counterfeit twenty-dollar bill.

A police officer knelt on Floyd's neck for eight minutes and forty-six seconds. The prejudice that underlies these moments of racialized police violence is reprehensible, but the disparities that lead to them are harder to recognize. It turns my stomach to think that the US hasn't dealt with bias enough to stop the unlawful killing of Black people at the hands of law enforcement. At the same time, in a country that sees such enormous wealth, it's also shameful that there are economic disparities that would motivate the circumstances for which police would be called at all.

In a country full of thriving industries, Floyd was also a man shut out from employment opportunities. While the country's richest citizens report record profits, there are people who struggle to scrape together twenty dollars. When the private sector voiced support for Black Lives Matter, many discussed police brutality, bias, and inequality. But instances of officers abusing their authority happen when responding to calls that are related to poverty. Biases compel some officers to make decisions in a specific encounter. At the same time, biases also drive entire industries to exclude Black people from socially acceptable forms of income in ways that make them more likely to be suspected of crime that requires law enforcement in the first place. While companies call out structural racism, they must also look at how business has the potential to stop it.

Beyond demanding justice for George Floyd's death, there is the economic justice that could have improved his life. In addition to calling for officers to be held accountable for how they treat Black suspects, businesses can combat the poverty that makes Black people seem suspicious in the first place. I am angry about how the police officers abused their power in ways that killed a Black man, but I wonder how much could be avoided altogether if organizations used their power to improve the lives of Black people. How much would counterfeit bills disappear? How much would the suspicions of shop owners dissipate? How many fewer calls to the police would be made? How much would racialized police violence, crime, poverty, unemployment, education gaps, income inequality, and healthcare disparities disappear? How much would Black lives improve if all the employers who said they supported Black Lives Matter movements started recruiting, hiring, onboarding, retaining, and mentoring like they knew Black lives matter?

This chapter will explore ways to make the arguments that will help organizations align their actions with their words. In many cases, creating a more inclusive company or business doesn't require radical changes as much as finding ways to help leaders simply become who they promised to be.

Understanding the Roadblocks to DEI

Workplace DEI requires consensus building. For inclusive policies to work, organizations need buy-in from multiple stakeholders. The programs that succeed are those that gain support at all levels. If we are to make persuasive arguments that DEI is even in the self-interest of its opponents, we must first understand its counterarguments.

To begin that process, we'll do an exercise I call "Build a Bridge." Get a large piece of paper, preferably a poster board. Title the poster "Bridge." Beneath that title, make four columns with plenty of space between them. Title the second column "Opposition to DEI." In it, **list all the reasons you have heard or can imagine hearing that oppose workplace DEI. Take some time now to come up with as many as possible.**

This list helps us appreciate the arguments against diversity, equity, and inclusion, but to understand them more fully, we must also understand the values that drive these arguments. Practice this by titling the first column of your table "Value." Match each opposition to DEI with the motivation that creates it. For example, if one argument is "it will cost us money," the motivation for it might be "financial stability." If another is "DEI will lower quality," the drive behind it might be "professional standards." Take some time. Think critically. Think creatively. Without judgment, with all fairness, reconstruct the most accurate set of values that might motivate arguments against DEI.

Chances are that most of your motivations fall into two broad categories: financial and moral. While arguments against this work can differ from one iteration to the next, they most commonly relate to concerns regarding whether DEI is the smart thing to do or the right thing to do. To earn the buy-in needed to gain support, we will now explore ways to appeal to these values.

The Financial Case for Inclusion

You might want to foster a more inclusive workplace but find yourself stalled by gatekeepers who cling to financial counterarguments. They might insist that they run a business, not a charity. They may claim that social issues like racial equity have no place in private enterprise. Most often, they'll imply that striving to be more just will erode quality and fill the employment roster with unqualified diversity hires. They'll mention words like "qualifications" to justify not seeing how qualified people of color can be. They'll insist they just focus on the facts and hire "the best person for the job" without considering a situation where a member of an underrepresented group might be the best person for the job. They'll insist they run a meritocracy without seeing how many of their behaviors ignore the merits of marginalized people. In these cases, some will dismiss moral arguments for inclusivity and require financial ones. When they do, here are some facts.

1. PROFITABILITY

For starters, inclusion is financially beneficial because it improves **profitability**. Stefanie K. Johnson is an associate professor at the University of Colorado Boulder's Leeds School of Business. In *Inclusify: The Power of Uniqueness and Belonging to Build Innovative Teams*, she examines the benefits of more inclusive workspaces. She finds that groups are 25 percent more likely to invest successfully when their team has racial diversity.

In addition to diversifying their teams, businesses hoping to thrive in the twenty-first century will have to diversify their customer base. About thirty-two million millennials in the United States identify as Asian, Black, or Hispanic. In 2021, African Americans represented a $1.5 trillion market. To appeal to the next generation of consumers, partners, vendors, and talent, companies must take proactive steps to show they value inclusion as much as this emerging demographic.

In 2015, a McKinsey Global Institute report found increased inclusivity could add $12 trillion to global GDP. In September 2020, Citi GPS found that more racial inclusion could have gained the US $16 trillion. If higher education had been more ethnically diverse, profits could have increased between $90 billion and $113 billion. If businesses had more justly paid African Americans, the economy would have seen an infusion of $2.7 trillion. Finally, if banks more fairly lent to Black entrepreneurs, the US economy could have gained $13 trillion in potential revenue. Beyond increased reach, inclusive organizations are 120 percent more likely to achieve their financial target goals because of greater morale and employee engagement.

2. QUALITY

In addition to increasing profits, greater inclusion helps organizations attract better workers and improve **quality**. The World Economic Forum projects that millennials will take up three quarters of the global workforce in the next few years and most leadership roles in the following decade. The 2020 Deloitte millennial survey found that three quarters of millennials insist diversity and inclusion are fundamental to innovation. Respondents went on to say that when seeking employers, the best and brightest consider a company's stance on diversity. For the first time since 2016, the 2020 survey found that more millennials said they would "like to stay with their employers for at least 5 years than would prefer to leave within 2 years." This remarkable spike in job loyalty comes when "businesses address employees' needs" and chief among them remains "diversity and inclusion." Beyond attracting the most qualified employees, greater diversity improves quality by creating the environment for better decision-making. It helps mitigate biases and produce broader thinking, considering new solutions and unexplored avenues that homogeneous teams overlook. With greater inclusion, teams are more likely to slow down, explain their thinking, and improve accuracy by 30 percent. While members of homogeneous organizations might feel more comfortable with one another, heterogeneous ones are more innovative.

3. MARKETABILITY

Besides improving profitability and quality, DEI helps organizations increase their **marketability**. A recent Edelman Earned Brand study showed that in 2017 only 13 percent of consumers would "choose, switch, avoid or boycott a brand based on where it stands on the political or social issues they care about." But in 2018, that same study found the number of belief-driven buyers in thirty-five countries jumped to 64 percent. The most lucrative emerging international markets, such as China, Brazil, and India, have the most people who engage in this consumer activism. Even US markets with relatively neutral customers have seen their numbers climb past 59 percent. With more than half the market looking for their consumer choices to perform some kind of ethical good, marketers have realized that the moral imperative to fight for social issues also carries a business imperative to take a stance. Inclusive companies increase their likelihood of reaching new markets by 70 percent. This statistic is changing quickly even when it comes to controversial issues. For example, when NFL quarterback Colin Kaepernick started kneeling during the national anthem in 2016, 20 percent of Americans supported athlete activism, but by 2020 that number had jumped to 70 percent. Furthermore, 70 percent say teams and leagues should both support BLM protests and initiatives as well as create marketing campaigns to support diversity.

4. DURABILITY

Some worry that embracing DEI will cause them to lose market share. The reluctant point to political groups that have threatened boycotts or legislation to punish companies that have taken a stance on social issues favoring underrepresented social identity groups. While the threats can be intimidating, the consumer backlash remains relatively small.

One reason why companies that embrace DEI don't suffer major losses is that statistics suggest opponents don't boycott as much as they insist they will. In "Who Actually Boycotts Brands?," Christopher Zara, a senior staff news editor for Fast Company, found that 43 percent of liberal consumers have boycotted a brand, while only 32 percent of conservatives claim the same.

Nailya Ordabayeva, associate professor of marketing at Boston College, notes that consumers from different political positions don't necessarily wield the same power over company profit. For example, in 2018, after the mass shooting at Marjory Stoneman Douglas High School, Dick's Sporting Goods decided to discontinue sales of semi-automatic weapons. Gun buyers vowed to boycott, but stock prices rose and "public perception of the brand is more positive overall." Fans warned NASCAR that if it got woke, it would go broke. But the sport with a Whiter, more conservative audience and deep connections to Confederate culture banned the Confederate flag, allowed Bubba Wallace to drive a car with BLACK LIVES MATTER painted on it, and embraced greater racial inclusion. Despite the promise of boycotts, the organization has held to these changes and experienced minimal financial impact. In all these cases, customers who threaten to walk away from companies that embrace DEI either lose their follow-through or have less economic impact than anticipated. In any case, most indicators suggest the financial fears leaders have about adopting DEI measures are unfounded.

5. VIABILITY

Even in situations when companies do experience a revenue dip for embracing inclusion, they persevere because of long-term investment strategies. For example, after Nike began airing commercials starring Colin Kaepernick, shares fell. While it's difficult to know whether those losses tie directly to one commercial, Nike stood by the decision to have the activist athlete represent the brand because "they always saw it as a way to engage with a younger audience" with more disposable income and higher potential for greater long-term brand loyalty that supports DEI more than their older counterparts.

Many other high-profile organizations, like the NFL, the NBA, and MLB, have taken public stances regarding racial justice that were controversial. DEI opponents warned that these organizations would see their profits plummet, but it appears that in most cases whatever losses come from people boycotting inclusive companies are minimal compared with the gains they attract from consumers supporting them. Even when these choices to embrace DEI result in losses, they appear to be part of an intentional long-term strategy designed to attract the markets of the future that have more spending power than those of the past.

6. PROVABILITY

While some critics dismiss DEI as a politically driven agenda, the scholarship shows it is a data-driven business decision. If you hope to appeal to detractors who cite business concerns, raise the business case. If they claim inclusivity measures will harm profit, quality, or market share, provide research on how DEI relates to those factors. Speak the language of stakeholders and meet them where they are. If their vocabulary is centered on statistics, shift your focus. If they're concentrated on financial issues, make financial arguments for DEI.

To make the alliances necessary to grow inclusion, you must be willing to build a bridge.

As part of that process, spend some time doing even more research on your own. Look for credible, peer-reviewed, or academic studies on how specific forms of diversity, equity, and inclusion affect business in general as well as your industry in particular. Crunch whatever data necessary to project how greater inclusivity would affect your specific business.

Many have strong opinions about DEI without many facts. Most of their impressions are rooted in ideological generalizations that are inaccurate. Step away from the rhetoric and look at the research. Explore the facts and cite them, especially with stakeholders who think none exist. When working with stakeholders who resist this work for financial reasons, claiming, for example, they "don't think business is any place for politics," dive into the pool of data regarding the financial case for DEI and show how, among all the other things it is, DEI is also a sound business strategy.

Evidence Exercise

Return to your Bridge. Title the third column "Evidence." Now, look at the Value column. For each item that mentions a value related to business, profit, or finances, go to the Evidence column. Use it to provide data from either this chapter or your own research that addresses those concerns. For example, if you wrote in the Opposition column the argument that "DEI will undermine quality," and you wrote in the Value column next to it that a person who makes this argument values "professional quality," go to the Evidence column and cite information from research about the steps a business must take to improve the quality of decision-making through heterogeneous groups. **Take time to write evidence that addresses counterarguments driven by business values.**

Limits of the Financial Case

While the business case is important, it isn't enough. In "Why the 'Business Case' for Diversity Isn't Working," Sarah Kaplan notes that leaders who are convinced by the business case alone might not see DEI's benefits. Some are attracted by nothing but the prospect of immediate, unequivocal, and steep increased revenue. They might even go so far as to recruit people from underrepresented groups. But the second they don't see quick gains, they scrap their inclusion projects. Kaplan points out that diversifying a workforce can produce initial dips in efficiency, productivity, and profitability as the team experiences change. While the organization adjusts, this initial dip can be enough to send some self-professed allies running for the door.

Economist Robin J. Ely and psychologist David A. Thomas make a similar argument. They note that the business case for DEI tempts business leaders to assume simply adding underrepresented people to their workforce will "*automatically* produce benefits." But they point out that taking this kind of "add diversity and stir approach, while business continues as usual, will not spur leaps in [a] firm's effectiveness or financial performance." They conclude that "what matters is how an organization harnesses diversity, and whether it's willing to reshape its power structure." Beyond passively opening themselves up to the possibility of greater diversity, successful companies are those that make the moral commitment to equity and inclusion that make the benefits of diversity possible.

Leaders who are convinced by the financial case for DEI alone won't endure financial difficulties long enough to see their rewards. To experience these benefits, they have to develop the fortitude to go beyond simply hiring for diversity and start changing their systems in ways that are more likely to make them uncomfortable. For these reasons, the financial case for DEI must be accompanied by a moral one.

The Moral Case

Some techniques for the moral approach survey the past. Historical and sociological arguments show the roots of racial inequality and have convinced many to recognize their indebtedness to this past and rectify the injustices that have benefited them. Ibram X. Kendi's *How to Be an Antiracist*, Robin DiAngelo's *White Fragility: Why It's So Hard for White People to Talk about Racism*, and Ijeoma Oluo's *So You Want to Talk about Race* look at the ways in which the past informs racism in the present. These works, along with others like Layla Saad's *Me and White Supremacy*, Jennifer Harvey's *Raising White Kids: Bringing Up Children in a Racially Unjust America*, and Tim Wise's *White Like Me*, have helped millions trying to understand their world in the aftermath of racialized police violence. In offices, churches, and virtual meeting rooms across the world, book clubs began discussing works like Michelle Alexander's *The New Jim Crow* and Ta-Nehisi Coates's *Between the World and Me* for the ways they put today's racial issues in historical context.

Other situations, however, might call for additional methods. There are plenty who reject links between historical injustices and business inequities. When it comes to the private sector, some have taken bold steps to address the connections between discrimination and their businesses, but there are more who have not and plenty who never will. Many cannot tie the current fiscal state of their organization to a historically documented moment where they sold babies away from their wailing mothers to improve a company's bottom line. In these situations, it becomes difficult to persuade business leaders that they have benefited from exclusion and been a major cause of it, and thus, for them to see the moral case for DEI.

So how can one circumvent these obstacles to convince stakeholders to adopt more inclusive policies? If the financial case for DEI falters unless it accompanies the moral case, and many dismiss historical and social arguments, what other approaches can increase buy-in?

Moral Opportunity

Many approaches to DEI focus on problems: antibias training concentrates on the psychological problem of bias, prejudice, and bigotry; and approaches to organizational management tend to focus on the problems of microaggressions, discrimination, and exclusionary behavior. Similarly, some moral arguments for DEI can accentuate guilt and obligation, but this approach relies on being able to convince people they are responsible for wrongdoing. If a leader, executives, or the entire organization rejects this responsibility, this kind of moral argument fails.

However, there are some other techniques. For example, instead of confining duty to situations where people must redress the evils they've done, your particular situation might require you to widen duty to also include moral opportunities where people can offer improvements they're uniquely positioned to provide. In doing so, you can also remind them of the good that they've promised to do. One such opportunity is something that I call the internal approach.

The Internal Approach

The internal approach focuses on the commitments that organizations have already made and simply challenges those entities to fulfill their promises. It concentrates on connections between what businesses say and what they do.

Businesses make all kinds of promises—those to their customers, clients, competitors, employees, shareholders, board members, legal authorities, and themselves. The internal approach to the moral argument for DEI hinges on what organizations say. In countless consulting situations, I've seen the most success when we focus on this internal approach. Many resist changes that seem inorganically forced upon them. Cookie-cutter techniques and generic rationales produce initiatives that falter or, even worse, never get off the ground.

Conversely, those that see the greatest successes seem to come from within the organization itself. Instead of trying to achieve compliance by imposing universal standards of what everyone should be, the internal approach seeks to inspire participation by investigating the internal standards of what organizations profess to be. It asks companies the following:

- What have you promised?
- How does DEI relate to that promise?
- How can DEI help you fulfill that promise?

Rather than holding businesses up to some universal moral standard, we'll look at the moral standards they set for themselves in all kinds of statements, proclamations, and publicity.

Cognitive Consistency

This internal approach to DEI relies on the desire humans feel to walk the walk. Human psychology abhors hypocrisy. Facing gaps between what one says and does causes severe emotional distress. To avoid this anguish, humans go to great lengths to change their behavior to match their words.

The title of this book references the proverb "Actions speak louder than words." Similar adages like "Talk is cheap" convey a collective wisdom that humans strive to bring their deeds in line with their speech. The entirety of contractual law that provides the foundation for social interactions operates off the assumption that people must do what they say. Facets of human experience from folk sayings to the legal bedrock of social groupings to the cornerstone of religions appeal to the almost primordial drive human beings have to fulfill promises.

For this reason, a central aspect of the moral argument for DEI hinges on these promises. In the summer of 2020, many companies made public declarations about the importance of racial justice. Not even eight days after George Floyd was murdered, all kinds of companies all over the US retweeted, hashtagged, and issued public promises that they would make changes to be more inclusive. After making these promises, true leaders feel the need to fulfill them.

Social psychologists Bertram Gawronski and Fritz Stack explore this deep motivation to line up actions with our promises. According to them, the "hypocrisy paradigm" emphasizes "the rational side of dissonance reduction ('Practice what you preach')." Beyond guilt-tripping people into doing what they said they'd do, this approach also nudges people into modified behavior that helps them "bring their behavior in line with attitudes and beliefs to which *they already subscribe*." To motivate people to change their behavior in ways that will sustain inclusion practices, you must create chances for reluctant leaders to see how DEI helps fulfill their need for cognitive consistency. Some ways to achieve this include the following:

1. REFLECT

Research the declarations of your organization by pulling up the posts and public statements it has made regarding commitments to inclusivity. Even if your business has never made a statement you think is even remotely related to DEI, it probably has a vision, mission, values statement, employee handbook, HR manual, or code of conduct. These documents function like a contract between the company and its stakeholders. By issuing this contract, the business promises to fulfill these terms. By showing up to work every day, team members agree to adhere to them. Given the weight of these documents, think of them as your company's constitution, and ensure any DEI proposal addresses these founding documents and reflects their values.

2. CONNECT

In addition to reflecting what the organization promises to be, a key element of making the moral argument is to show leaders how DEI helps them connect to their promises. A study of hundreds of statements that articulated company values found diversity was the ninth most common. Even if your company doesn't mention this particular concept, the top three values are respect, customer service, and teamwork. Each of these are fundamental to DEI and significantly aided by it. Rather than thinking of DEI as some new idea opposed to your company's values, show how it is a key element that has always undergirded them. Whatever your situation, consider your company's value statement as the promise your organization made that justifies all other DEI work stemming from it. Conversely, every inclusivity program you want to implement should have a direct line back to it. Like an attorney appearing before the US Supreme Court, be prepared with arguments that are constitutionally justified. If some claim a program, policy, or procedure is a radical violation of that founding document, have evidence that it actually conforms to it. When we plan the DEI objectives we'll explore later in the book, a fundamental part of making the moral argument is ensuring they aren't impositions as much as amendments.

3. DIRECT

Beyond reflecting and connecting, the most successful moral arguments are those that demonstrate to leaders how DEI helps them direct their promises. After showing the organization what it has promised to be and how greater inclusivity can help fulfill that promise, explain how those measures can also create even more opportunity. The "direct" portion of the moral argument shows how DEI can help the organization realize its moral opportunities more than ever before. It goes beyond the "reflect" and "connect" strategies that illustrate how DEI matches who they already are. The "direct" aspect shows how DEI can reveal aspects of their identity they never knew were there.

Now, Build a Bridge

Return to your Bridge. Look at the Value column. For each item that mentions a value related to morality, politics, the organization's identity, or relevance, go to the Evidence column. In that column, provide data from either this chapter or your own research into your organization's constitution that addresses each concern.

Maybe you wrote in the Opposition column the argument that "DEI is political and has no place here." Perhaps you wrote in the Value column next to it that a person who makes this argument values "professional relevance." Then you might go to the Evidence column and cite information from your organization's values statement that promises, "We treat everyone with respect." Then show how DEI is professionally relevant to fulfilling this constitutional value and can help the organization achieve this goal even more fully. **Take time to write evidence that addresses counterarguments driven by moral values.**

The Bridge you've developed throughout the exercises in this chapter provides the outline for arguments that will help convince your organization to adopt DEI initiatives. Each row contains a particular set of values, opposition, and evidence that will maximize your persuasiveness. On the far right, title the fourth column "Proposal." As we go throughout this book, you'll find suggestions for specific actions. For example, the chapter on mentoring could make you want to propose your organization's first mentorship program. Great! Create a clear bridge from one supporting beam to the next. Come to this big chart and insert all the connections that would link the proposal back to the evidence, opposition, and values of your organization.

As you go throughout this book, constantly return to your Bridge, and insert all the supports you can imagine. Don't propose anything unless you can draw a clear chain between a particular proposal and a core value of your organization. Before assembling a DEI task force, draw out a link of circles and lines that shows how that proposed task force would fulfill x that fulfills y that fulfills z that fulfills a financial value that's foundational to the organization. Before thinking about issuing a DEI statement, create a bridge of supports that shows how the statement would fulfill a that fulfills b that fulfills c that fulfills a moral value that's essential to the identity your company claims to have. For example, if your company has a core value of respect, show how the DEI task force would exist to conduct surveys, focus groups, and listening sessions to see how well people from the most commonly disrespected social groups think the company can live up to that value even more.

The chapters that follow concentrate on specific things like recruiting, hiring, onboarding, retention, mentoring, meetings, and performance reviews. But all the narrow professional elements we'll cover require the broader financial and moral evidence you've created in your Bridge. To make changes, you must earn buy-in. You can't impose changes that demand compliance. To achieve the sustainability that produces genuine inclusion, you must create the conditions through which even the most resistant can see how DEI is in their own self-interest.

Use the values, opposition, and evidence you've mapped to develop the proposals that show how adopting DEI principles will help your organization fulfill both its financial goals and its moral opportunities. Use these exercises to explain how DEI reflects who they already are. Connect to opponents' promises in ways that help fulfill them, and direct them into the future, where they can achieve the promises more fully than they ever imagined. To acquire the participation necessary to change, you must appreciate opposition. Anticipate, understand, and know it. Learn it inside and out. Then build a bridge.

PART II

Organizational
Development

CHAPTER FOUR

Recruiting
"Minorities Just Don't Apply Here"

I was attending a discussion on the value of diversity in higher education. We sat in the large seminar room complete with swivel chairs and pitchers of water as presentations flickered on the projector screen citing a parade of facts and figures. Everyone agreed it was important to have diversity, create equitable structures to promote it, and find ways to make their respective institutions as inclusive as possible. While all the participants nodded in agreement, they also shrugged their shoulders in resignation.

A man with a white beard and elbow patches articulated what all the dour-faced participants already knew. He cleared his throat and congratulated the fifth presenter for piling more data on top of plenty, preaching to the choir that DEI was important, virtuous, and beneficial. But then he said, "Too bad minorities just don't apply here."

At that precise moment, the world beyond that room decided to encroach upon it as the walls shook with laughter. The man with the white beard scowled at the intrusion. The others joined in, clenching jaws and shifting in their seats as if they were the object of the chuckles.

The man went on to explain that due to a scheduling conflict, the adjacent room was full of hundreds of high school juniors celebrating their final day of a yearlong program designed to help students from underrepresented groups prepare for college.

There I had been sitting all morning, listening to one leader after another talk about the importance of diversity only to have them throw up their hands in resignation, assuming they could never achieve their lofty goals because "minorities just don't apply here," and then bristle at the hundreds of members from that target demographic enjoying pizza, soda, and graduation speeches just one room over!

I've seen different versions of this story happen dozens of times. In each, an organization declares its desire to be more inclusive. Its leaders wonder why the populations they seek don't come to their room but never think to get up and walk one door over. To everyone who's established all kinds of DEI initiatives only to wonder, "Why aren't underrepresented communities coming to us?" I ask, "Why aren't you going to them?"

Hampten Institute

Imagine there's a new Hampten Institute that took students with high scores in the areas of resiliency, creativity, and adaptability and gave them interdisciplinary education that fostered their capacity for generating innovative ideas. Now let's imagine 67 percent of employees say that when evaluating prospective employers, they wanted to know how many Hampten graduates the company employed. Imagine consulting groups found that businesses with an above-average number of Hampten graduates could expect to have 45 percent average higher innovation revenue essential to generating the new products, markets, and industries at the heart of the multitrillion-dollar creative economy. Finally, imagine global analysts project that by 2025, Hampten graduates would give the US economy a $5 trillion boost.

With this information, would you hold meetings to discuss the virtues of hiring Hampten graduates? If no one from that institute applied for a job with your organization, would you shrug and say, "Too bad Hampten graduates just don't apply here"? Realizing the potential of this demographic, would you even wait around long enough for them to graduate before approaching them? The answer to all these questions is probably a resounding no. Sixty-seven percent of employees suggesting they would work only with employers that also hired Hampten grads, 45 percent more innovation revenue, and $5 trillion! Looking at those statistics, most leaders wouldn't wait for graduates to apply, they would seek them out.

To see how this is the case, let's do a little exercise. Title a piece of paper or document "Hampten Institute Plan." What would you do to draw graduates from this place of higher learning? Think proactively. Think competitively. Attracting this group before other organizations do may be the precise thing that helps your organization thrive—maybe even survive. With these stakes in mind, **list all the things you would do to recruit a Hampten Institute graduate.**

Before the first set of Hampten students even walked across the graduation stage, most employers would find ways to create partnerships with the institute. They would establish internships with competitive salaries and compile packages of perks. Employers would create a situation where it seemed as if they were submitting their application to the employee instead of the other way around. Businesses would sponsor career fairs, work with the institute's career services department, and create a mentorship program between current employees and prospective ones from Hampten. Companies would devise elaborate value propositions for Hampten students even in their junior year, eager to secure agreements with people long before their final exams. At the very least, employers would send an email to the Hampten Institute to advertise the latest open positions. Why? Business leaders would see those numbers—67 percent employability, 45 percent more innovation revenue, $5 trillion—and would unleash the full resources of their business to recruit Hampten graduates before they even had to complete a single job application.

African Americans

After you list strategies for the Hampten Institute Plan, think about DEI resistance. Imagine you're trying to develop a more diverse team. For our purposes, we'll concentrate on African American employees. Think about all the counterarguments people would pose if you wanted to recruit African Americans to your organization.

When I've done this exercise in the past, participants have noted that they would face questions about why an organization would spend time or money on "special recruitments," insistence that the company's hiring practices are fine so there's no need to change them, declarations that the organization is a meritocracy and should wait for the most qualified members to present themselves, all kinds of excuses that there just aren't any in the industry—and, of course, the common refrain: "Too bad minorities just don't apply here."

Compare and contrast the strategy to recruit Hampten graduates with the situation that arises when it comes to hiring African Americans. It is interesting to see the types of creative ideas leaders will devise, extraordinary things leaders will do, and the staggering resources they'll deploy to attract the former. At the same time, there is often the same amount of creativity put into developing reasons why a company shouldn't take simple steps to recruit the latter. This contrast becomes even starker given the fact that Hampten Institute in this exercise is fictionalized. There are no Hampten graduates who employees are clamoring to work with, who can increase profits, and who could boost the market. But there is a group that is linked to improved employee recruitment, innovation, and market share.

It is not Hampten graduates but employees from underrepresented populations that attract 76 percent of prospective employees. It is not students from a fictional institute but team members from marginalized communities that help raise innovation revenues by 45 percent. One might feel sadness upon learning that there is no set of alumni from a made-up institution of higher learning that could infuse the US economy with trillions of dollars, but African Americans are a real group that has that potential. So the question remains: Why are so many able to come up with methods for attracting fabricated graduates of a fictional university because of their imaginary benefits and not actual Black people with their real benefits?

Take a moment to think deeply, and write some answers to this question.

Despite these statistics about the importance of DEI when it comes to hiring, countless organizations sit on the sidelines, changing nothing about their recruiting process yet expecting things to change. How can some suggest they would be inclusive leaders if only they came across an application from a single "minority"? How can they believe they'll ever receive such an application, especially when their competitors are already making the necessary changes and will leave them behind when it comes to recruiting from underrepresented groups? How can they not see the lack of Black people who apply for jobs at their organization as an implicit indictment of how exclusive the organization is or how much it fails to communicate its inclusive values? What do they think the situation will look like a decade from now? If your competitors have already made the changes to be more inclusive today, by contrast, how much more homogeneous will your employee roster look when you're trying to attract people from under-represented groups ten years from now?

To begin making moves so the demographics of your organiza-tion begin reflecting those of the customer market, talent pool, and world of the future, there are a few recruiting strategies you can use.

Steps for Inclusivity

1. MULTIPLY THE NUMBER OF PEOPLE WHO WRITE YOUR JOB ADVERTISEMENTS.

Every decision a person makes has an assumed outcome in mind. One's presuppositions limit the questions they'll ask, the places they'll search, and the things they'll consider. If you haven't fully ar-ticulated the job advertisement, you are operating off a lot of defaults. Because the mind gravitates toward the familiar, there's a high probability that the default employee it wants to hire is a carbon copy of the kinds of employees that populate most organizations.

If you want to multiply your productivity and profitability, you want to multiply the kind of thinking that appears on your team. To hire someone who will think of things that you can't, seek them with an advertisement written by a bunch of people who already think differently from you. Even if it seems like the simplest paragraph that should take five minutes to write, assemble a group of people. The purpose of hiring someone is to add to your organization something that you can't. You don't want to hire twenty versions of you. Multiplying the types of thoughts that arise from your company requires you to multiply the number of people who write the job advertisement to which these prospective multipliers would respond.

2. DIVERSIFY THE BACKGROUNDS OF JOB ADVERTISEMENT WRITERS.

With more people on the committee, you'll gain a broader perspective, but you can acquire an even wider view if those people come from different social groups. If you want greater diversity in your organization, start with having greater diversity on the committee that writes the job descriptions that are supposed to attract people to your organization. While diversifying your committee of writers is likely to make your job ad more inclusive, this result isn't guaranteed. Of course, it's reductive to assume that a person of color will automatically have views that are drastically different from those of a White person. It can be insulting to assume that a woman naturally has profound opinions about how to write job ads that will automatically attract women.

But leaders increase the likelihood that they will attract diverse talent if they have diverse committees writing the ads to attract them. They can increase the chances that they'll catch an exclusionary phrase to remove or a more inviting tone to include. If your team doesn't already have members from the groups you want to hire, hire DEI consultants to look through your job advertisements. Whatever you do, if you want applicants from different backgrounds, make sure you have job ad writers from different backgrounds.

3. REMOVE BIASED LANGUAGE.

Before respondents submit their application to you, you are marketing to them. In a short job advertisement, you try to make your organization sound like a place worth joining. It becomes especially important for you to scrutinize your ad for biased language that suggests the underrepresented people you seek won't discard your post as representing organizations that are as racist, sexist, homophobic, transphobic, classist, ableist, or ageist as the rest. If you're wondering why people from underrepresented groups aren't responding to your postings, examine the vocabulary those ads use. Studies show that biased language in job advertisements is a major reason why people ignore certain jobs. There might be nothing morally "wrong" with words like "determine," "aggressive," "competitive," "execute," "capture," "analyze," "drive," and "individual." However, they might be rhetorically ineffective when trying to attract marginalized communities. Why? US society heavily codes these characteristics as the property of straight, White, cisgender, non-disabled men, and research shows that people who don't belong to this demographic tend to subconsciously take these words as cues that the job being advertised isn't for them.

4. REVISE TITLES.

This problem with vocabulary also applies to the titles your advertisements use. If your goal is to diversify your pool of candidates, avoid clearly gendered terms like "guys," "policeman," "fireman," "chairman," "salesman." Even reconsider words that aren't obviously gendered but evoke positions heavily coded as masculine: "hacker," "rock star," "superhero." If you're scratching your head, wondering why people of color ignore your postings, double-check that those blurbs you're sending out into the world avoid language that evoke a history of violent ethnocentrism like "pioneer" or "master." Resist the tendency to flippantly appropriate important aspects of other cultures for exaggerated metaphors of professional tenacity like "ninja" or "guru."

5. RECONSIDER UNNECESSARY COMPARISONS.

Psychologists Jessi L. Smith and Meghan Huntoon found that modesty norms discourage women from self-promoting. The case is similar for people from other underrepresented groups who have been taught that the professional world is for people who look different from them. Living in a society that projects a certain picture of victors, marginalized people often decide not to apply for jobs with descriptions that emphasize competition and ranking. Therefore, words like "premier," "preeminent," "superior," "world-class," "expert," "dominant," "top," and "high-ranked" cause problems. If the goal is to describe a job, they're unnecessary. Oftentimes, they are the product of advertisers' compulsion to exaggerate their own importance. Beyond being unnecessary and self-serving, they have the unintended consequence of telling potential candidates that the position is intended for "winners" and will likely attract only social groups that society has stereotyped as such.

6. SHORTEN LISTS OF QUALIFICATIONS.

As you're drafting your post, you'll feel the urge to confuse that document with a wish list. As your imagination runs away from you, the list of ideal characteristics will grow longer and longer. There's nothing wrong with dreaming big, but listing all these aspirations in an advertisement will have certain effects. Nancy F. Clark, CEO of PositivityDaily, finds that men apply for jobs when they meet 60 percent of the qualifications, but women wait until they meet 100 percent. From this data, author Tara Sophia Mohr concludes that the more requirements a job advertisement lists, the more men will apply compared with the number of women. Suspecting the professional sphere already isn't designed with them in mind, marginalized people will be more likely to experience the insecurity that accompanies impostor syndrome. When marginalized people receive countless messages that they don't belong, long lists of qualifications can evoke this feeling and keep certain people from ever applying at all.

7. USE RECRUITMENT TECHNIQUES THAT CENTRALIZE UNDERREPRESENTED COMMUNITIES.

Beyond revising job advertisements, don't simply wait for people from underrepresented groups to apply. Rather than wait for them to come to your room, go to theirs. Do what you would do with Hampten Institute graduates. Do what you would do if you fully appreciated how frequently many of your competitors that have diverse teams are already doing these things. Consider the fact that one reason underrepresented people aren't applying to your organization is that other organizations are recruiting them before diverse candidates ever get the chance.

Target your recruiting efforts to the few areas of the world where the underrepresented are represented. Whether it's attending the annual conference of the National Black Law Students Association or a meeting of the Association for Women in Science, prove that you're willing to step out of your comfort zone and into theirs. Look at professional organizations, national associations, affinity groups, conferences, job fairs, and networking events of these diverse populations.

8. PROVE YOU ACTUALLY SUPPORT THOSE COMMUNITIES.

Many show up for a five-minute speech, set up a ten-foot table, or post an ad on the platform for twenty days. But you must demonstrate a commitment to the communities from which you seek to draw. Many of the associations for social groups that I talk to mention the current climate. Many companies have jumped on the DEI bandwagon. Unimaginative or insincere when it comes to being more inclusive, they all reach out to these identity-specific groups and ask them to post job advertisements.

The problem is that so many are exploiting this tactic. At best, they add job announcements to a heap that just produces static noise. At worst, they look like what many have taken to calling "poachers," supposed recruiters looking to nab a handful of minorities for the organizational photo shoot before setting them in a cubicle where they have no input, opportunities, or room for advancement.

There are plenty who want diverse talent but not diverse experiences or diverse thinking. Avoid looking like a performative ally who'll engage in exploitative tokenism and instead show that you are willing to listen. Demonstrate that you're not just going to steal from the community by instead proving you're willing to support it.

Instead of just making a speech, setting up a table, or posting an ad at an event for Reaching Out MBA, an organization that focuses on LGBTQ+ MBA communities, ask to sponsor an event. Partner with university DEI offices, underwrite virtual career fairs that focus on minority student groups, and work with current partners and vendors with members from marginalized communities for opportunities.

9. ARTICULATE YOUR ORGANIZATION'S DEI BRAND.

Rakuna, a human resources tech company, presses employers to consider their diversity brand. Organizations wouldn't market a product to a demographic without providing a clear sense of the company's identity. Similarly, companies need to realize that every organization has a brand that communicates volumes regarding its relationship to DEI. Among companies, the most common diversity brand is none at all, complete with no demonstrated commitment to the values of inclusion.

If your CEO hasn't issued a diversity statement, if your company doesn't articulate a plan to become more inclusive, if your website doesn't feature any of the company's DEI efforts—the absence of these things doesn't communicate neutrality. It communicates an active rejection of them. The absence of an intentional plan suggests that a company's members haven't given any thought to answering the question, "What have we done that would make marginalized people think this would be a place where they are welcome?" In all these situations, remember that you have suspicion to overcome and trust to gain. To prove your sincerity in the community, take time to be a part of it, invest in it, and sponsor it.

10. RETHINK YOUR CURRENT NETWORKS.

Many of the tips so far have talked about receiving applications from underrepresented people by recruiting in different circles, but the line between networks and diverse circles often overlaps. For many, the problem isn't that they have no networks with underrepresented communities as much as they simply don't think of those networks. Take inventory of your organization's ERGs, HR programs promoting diversity, or DEI offices. These avenues provide access to different social groups that many leaders often overlook. Executives might accept references for hires on the golf course, but they should also look for them in community partnerships. In these instances, leaders who seek to recruit more actively must simply widen their perspective to see the other affiliations they already have.

"Go One Room Over"

Back in that conference room where I had spent hours listening to people discuss the value of diversity in higher education, I responded to the laughter of the students differently. Most scowled at the wall, thinking the noise was a nuisance, but I saw a solution. When we took a break for lunch, I packed my things, left the room, and wandered into the neighboring one. Instead of spending the rest of the afternoon talking about how important students of color were, I decided to enjoy the rest of the day talking to some of them. I exchanged business cards, made connections, and devised strategies with them.

While I never returned to the first conference room, I continue to run into people like those who inhabited it. Even years later, people will sit through training sessions on the importance of DEI only to linger afterward to tell me they appreciated my lessons but don't know how they apply to their particular organization because . . . (you guessed it!) "minorities just don't apply here." It is at that moment that I reach for my phone full of contacts I made at that pizza party for high school juniors so many years ago. After I bombard them with more names, numbers, and résumé links than they could ever want, bewildered people often ask me how in the world they could ever hope to make all these connections. To which I answer, "Go one room over."

CHAPTER FIVE

Hiring
"This Is a No-Brainer"

A few years ago, I was asked to work with an organization that was looking to hire a new leader. The board was composed of mostly White, wealthy women, and they were choosing between two candidates: an African American woman we'll call Anitra and a White woman we'll call Wendy.

Anitra was an internal candidate who had been with the company for more than a decade. She ran all the main divisions of the company and was key in helping each division thrive. She graduated from a small, local college and had earned the respect of the team before the leader of the organization placed her as the top pick for the job.

Wendy was an external candidate who hadn't held an outside senior leadership role. Nevertheless, one of the board members was a longtime friend of hers and invited her to apply for the position.

When we debated the virtues of hiring either applicant, it struck me how many tangential factors became essential to our conversation. Of course, we covered the most pertinent issues—skills, experience, and character—to see which applicant would help take the organization forward. But buried in the many hours of conversation were two very striking comments.

The first was about Anitra. Long into our discussion, when it came time to consider how well each candidate would appeal to the organization's funders, one board member started slowly, talking about disposition and comportment before she mentioned that Anitra loved to wear bold colors, dyed her hair, and possibly lacked "executive presence."

The second comment that stood out was about Wendy. Another board member noted that she had known Wendy for a long time, they lived in the same neighborhood, and their kids had played together their entire lives—all evidence that she would be a great leader. Others added that as soon as they saw the institution Wendy graduated from, they knew she was the right fit, and the interview process only verified their initial "hunch."

After all the conversation about "executive presence" and "hunches," the board chair concluded the discussion, saying of the decision to hire Wendy, "This is a no-brainer." If I were not there to help point out some of what I share below, I am confident that the team would have missed how they were letting bias unfairly underrate Anitra.

While most hiring processes might not be as explicit about it, many feature this kind of "no-brainer" moment. Facing a mountain of résumés or a sea of hiring metrics, the quantitative data overwhelms, and the employer decides on a candidate because the hiring manager "has a good feeling." But the science shows that when people make hiring, interviewing, and selection choices based on hunches, they're usually operating off favoritism for people who resemble them.

Despite the overwhelming evidence about how pervasive bias is, there are employers who insist they transcend prejudice. Despite statistics about how common discrimination is, they insist they are logical, rational, and focused on the data.

For those who have an undying belief in their ability to be neutral, being asked to consider social identity when hiring can backfire. Perhaps you've looked at the need for your industry to branch out into international markets and suggested your employer should hire more immigrants only to have your company's hiring managers say it was unfair to consider non-job-related factors like nationality. Maybe you've simply suggested that interviewers put more women of color on the résumé screening committee, and they've said they didn't want to do anything political like factoring identity into the hiring process.

When facing those who swear they focus on "just the facts," there are particular arguments for inclusivity that can take them at their word and challenge them to narrow their focus even more. As this chapter will show, there are plenty of circumstances where those who claim to ignore identity actually fixate on it. If you're working with those who claim to be objective, we'll now explore methods for tightening the concentration even more strictly on "objective data" in each stage of the hiring process in ways that can prove surprisingly inclusive.

Hiring for the Status Quo

In my situation with Anitra and Wendy, the board made its decision based on a factor that plays a deciding role in many hiring processes. The choice to hire the latter became a "no-brainer" once the board established that Wendy would match their organization because she was like them. Other hiring committees might not be so blatant in the socioeconomic biases that constitute that match, but most essentially look for a candidate who will make for a good "culture fit." This habit can take on many forms. For some organizations, it means hiring people who look, act, and talk like their members. For others, it can refer to leaders who gravitate toward job candidates who share their values, personalities, and working styles. In most, however, it's a combination of both, with companies hiring candidates who conform to the professional culture of the business as well as the social cultures of that business's leaders.

Of course, the example of Anitra and Wendy shows how this drive can reinforce ethnocentric bias. At the same time, however, there are virtues to hiring for culture fit. In *The Psychology of Behaviour at Work*, occupational psychologist Adrian Furnham defines this "fit" as the "congruence between the norms and values of the organization and those of the person." Experimental psychologist and chief psychometrician at Good&Co., Kerry Schofield, notes that establishing culture fit is a good thing for both the organization and the individual, ensuring potential candidates will be happy in their new position.

However, problems await organizations that concentrate on culture fit too much. Content marketing specialist Bailey Reiners argues that when leaders hire only people who conform to their companies, they fall back on dangerous assumptions that prevent those entities from growing: "Working with people who continue to fit into a culture is not only a sure fire way to reinforce unconscious bias, but in the long run, it limits a team's ability to think creatively and generate innovative ideas and solutions."

This unconscious bias can take many forms and have many causes. For example, it might be an ethnocentric prejudice against Black-named applicants. But it's also a larger, more pervasive, and nuanced status quo bias against any kind of difference. I doubt the board members I worked with had a bigoted objection to hiring Anitra because they feared she would rob them or steal company property. Many résumé reviewers might avoid the bigoted bias that a Black employee would perform substandard work.

At the same time, however, there is another bias that favors the comfortable. People can fear others who are different, but they can also fear their own ability to engage with difference. "How can I make small talk, find common ground, and create common understanding with people who are so different? An applicant who self-identifies as gay? What if I accidentally say something homophobic? Official identification forms still list an applicant as 'female' although they now identify as 'male'? How am I supposed to act around a trans person when I've never even known one before? If Anitra wears bright colors and dyes her hair, what other personality differences exist between us? But Wendy? She dresses, looks, and lives like us."

At the end of the day, even those allies who've been through all the antibias training, read all the books, and attended all the marches can still end up making decisions that reinforce inequality. They can even hire in ways that disadvantage underrepresented people without ever "being racist," "bigoted," or even "biased" against women of color. Why? Because the status quo bias that makes the decision to hire Wendy a no-brainer seems to have nothing to do with social identity and has everything to do with what seems easier, more comfortable, and more fitting for the organization.

In "Are Emily and Greg More Employable Than Lakisha and

Jamal?," economists Marianne Bertrand and Sendhil Mullainathan responded to job advertisements with 2,435 résumés. They paired each application with similar relevant qualifications but changed the name of the job applicants. One set had names that suggested Black identity, like Aisha, Ebony, Darnell, and Hakim, while their corresponding pair had names that suggested White identity, like Kristen, Meredith, Neil, and Todd. They found that "White-named" applicants had a callback rate of 9.7 percent, while "Black-named" applicants had a callback rate of 6.5 percent. Given this disparity between responses to résumés based on nothing but the supposed racial identity of an applicant's name, Bertrand and Mullainathan concluded that their findings imply that a "White applicant should expect on average one callback for every 10 ads she or he applies to; on the other hand, an African American applicant would need to apply to 15 different ads to achieve the same result."

The same people who claim to be objective and focus on accomplishments instead of things like race and gender also look to elements of the standard résumé for clues to social identity. They might file lawsuits against affirmative action programs for asking applicants to reveal their racial or gender identity in ways that might benefit underrepresented groups, but they also use standard résumé elements like an applicant's name to weed out those who don't have the names of White men.

They might criticize hiring programs designed for economically disadvantaged groups, claiming they give unfair advantages to the unqualified, but they also use the names of an applicant's university as a shorthand for one's proximity to wealth. Opponents to "diversity hiring" might cry foul when applicants talk about their experience as a first-generation college student from a Black community, but studies show they also scour the more traditional details that appear in the special interests section of a résumé for hints about an applicant's social background.

In these situations, the problem can be that reviewers refuse to see more information, narrowing their vision so they can ignore things like race, gender, and class. At the same time, however, another problem is that they leave their vision wide enough to include things like applicant names, universities, and special interests that provide clues about those same social identities. They don't want hiring committees to ask for an applicant's race or gender in ways that could benefit people from underrepresented groups, but they still use something as simple as a name to determine an applicant's race or gender in ways that discriminate against them.

In this situation, there are a few tips.

Steps for Inclusivity

1. REDACT RÉSUMÉS.

When facing those who argue against considering social identity in evaluating applicants, a solution might be removing even more elements of identity. GapJumpers is a design company that takes résumés and removes information that can suggest the social identity of applicants. GapJumpers found that when employers use redacted résumés, women are 50 percent more likely to advance to the final rounds of hiring and about "60% of the top talent identified through GapJumpers' blind audition process come from underrepresented backgrounds."

When hirers remove things like name, university, and special interests, which can suggest the social identity of the applicant, they make decisions that are even more "objective" than DEI opponents claim they should be. These statistics suggest that those who claimed to hire people based on merit alone were making biased decisions all along. If your leaders claim to hire the most qualified people, challenge them to remove everything but the qualifications. When they do so, studies show their hiring ends up becoming more inclusive.

2. SPECIFY CRITERIA.

While redacted résumés are important to achieve the "objectivity" that makes more inclusion possible, it's important to also specify criteria used to evaluate which data to redact, which data to retain, and how to interpret the data that remains. In attempts to minimize hiring costs and increase efficiencies, many companies are turning to artificial intelligence. Management consulting group Korn Ferry reports that 88 percent of their respondents worked with recruitment outsourcing partners to investigate the internet for potential candidates. In 2018, 91 percent of tech companies put resources into sourcing tools, and 64 percent of talent acquisition professionals will budget money for AI-recruiting tools.

Behavioral and data scientist Pragya Agarwal examines the prevalence of bias in human cognition. She applauds the efforts of company leaders to circumvent their biases by using third parties or AI as part of the hiring process. However, she warns against the assumption that an outsourcing agency or AI system can avoid the biases of its employers. She notes that in 2018, Amazon developed an AI hiring tool to rank candidates according to the organization's past preferences. The promise was that this résumé-scanning tool could get around the biases that had plagued the company's hiring efforts.

However, problems arose when the system began automatically downgrading applications that contained feminine-coded language and upgrading those that contained masculine-coded language. Why? Because no matter how objective the AI system could ever be, it was still programmed by humans within an organization that hadn't fully interrogated its own biases. If your company wants to hire third parties or create software programs, it still must interrogate its hiring criteria.

If you don't have resources for these hiring techniques, the challenge remains. The point isn't that AI is flawed. The point is that AI is only as good as the criteria it receives. These statistics about AI just show that you must be clear about the criteria you're giving the recruiting team, whether that's a committee of twenty people or only you. Question and revise the programs you use to decide which résumés advance, whether you have an elaborate AI system or only your own mind.

3. CONSIDER QUESTIONNAIRES.

Beyond redaction and specified criteria, a third solution for a more inclusive résumé-review process is removing résumés altogether and using questionnaires. A fundamental flaw of résumé review is the assumption that the social identity of an applicant is synonymous with their work potential. Even when DEI advocates circumvent these biases, another one remains: the tendency to conflate approximation with attainment. Résumé reviewers presume that my graduating from a particular institution means I've learned the skills that university teaches; that my working at one company means I've practiced the skills that organization required; or that my having a particular reward, title, or position means I have the skills required of that professional identity. But education, work experience, and job titles don't necessarily indicate skills.

Many employers have pinpointed this problem and started challenging the traditional hiring process by using questionnaires. To a large extent, the purpose of hiring is to acquire the skills an individual can bring to an organization. Instead of posting a job advertisement with a list of qualification requirements, industry leaders are posting projects for potential applicants to complete. Instead of asking for a person's work experience, education, or even name, these kinds of questionnaires can cut everything but the information most directly related to the job.

If an organization wanted résumés to help it hire the best widget maker, why would it ask applicants for the names of their previous employers or educational backgrounds? During the initial stages of the review process, why would it even have to know their names? Instead, the organization could create project-based applications where applicants have an identification code and explain how they would make widgets or solve different problems. Of course, many positions have nonnegotiable requirements, but a questionnaire can answer these essential questions with a yes or no instead of open-ended ones that can lead to biases. For example, a questionnaire can ask, "Do you have a college degree?" without a résumé whose format expects applicants to say where they got their college degree. A questionnaire can ask, "Do you have X license?" without a résumé whose conventions dictate that applicants would say where they got that license.

Critics say DEI promotes undeserving applicants. According to them, instead of focusing on irrelevant identity information like an applicant's race, gender, and sexual orientation, résumé reviewers should concentrate on nothing but skills. If this is the case, they can forgo the traditional résumés in favor of limited questionnaires that focus on skills and ignore irrelevant identity information like an applicant's university, previous employers, affiliations, or name. Interestingly, when companies take this approach and strive to be even more objective than traditionalists, they find that applicants from underrepresented groups move to first-round interviews 40 percent more often.

4. HIRE FOR "CULTURE ADD."

These first three tips focus on anonymizing hiring materials, but making this process more inclusive also requires being intentional about hiring for difference. It becomes problematic if the highest goal of hiring for diversity is to hire people based on their social background. This approach sets organizations up to make clumsy hires and dooms people from underrepresented groups to a career of tokenism. Why? Because doing little more than trying to hire a bunch of people who look different doesn't do anything to ensure the organization will let them make the company different. The point of hiring for diversity isn't just to add different kinds of people to your roster. It's to add different kinds of experience, perspectives, ideas, and thinking to improve your organizational decision-making.

The companies that achieve this are willing to change. They understand that it doesn't make sense to post a job advertisement that seeks people who are different just to turn around and spend all its energy trying to hire someone who's the same. You can avoid social identity bias by going through DEI training, but you must also side-step status quo bias by doing some deep reflection.

> **To start thinking about ways to hire for culture add, journal some answers to the following questions:**
>
> - What are the homogeneities of your organization?
> - What are the shortcomings they create?
> - What clusters of sameness produce redundant thoughts and narrow focus?
> - What are the pinch points at your organization where everyone ends up thinking the same?
> - What are the cardinal assumptions no one would dare challenge or even question?
> - How do you want your organization to change and why?
> - What are the gaps in approaches to organizational decision-making?
> - What are the skills, characteristics, and personality traits of the ideal candidate who would fill in those gaps?

Go beyond looking for applicants who would assimilate into the organization; look for those who would make it evolve—even in uncomfortable, difficult, and challenging ways. In addition to addressing prejudices against people from different backgrounds, expose the prejudices for what's familiar, easy, and comfortable. Make it clear to yourself, your team, and your organization that the point of hiring shouldn't be a continuation of the status quo. The point of hiring should be to make the organization grow. Establish what it means for your business to go beyond the default practice of hiring for "culture fit" and start the work of hiring for "culture add."

Go beyond pinpointing the social identity of candidates that you assume will add to your culture. For example, if you're looking to expand into African American markets, setting out to hire Black talent isn't enough. Beyond having a Black person, you'd probably also want one who had deep ties to and understanding of these communities and who also had the grit, perseverance, and diplomatic skills to tactfully resist the Eurocentric assumptions of coworkers. For these reasons, make part of your criteria for culture add go beyond social identity to include the specific social skills that will help ensure that underrepresented experiences, perspectives, and ideas become a part of the organization's decision-making.

Write down the criteria for the culture adds that you'd like to see now.

5. RESTRUCTURE INTERVIEWING TO REQUIRE CULTURE ADD.

Alex Moore is senior director, head of talent at Credera. She notes that employers who interview for culture add change their approach. They focus on skills but also behaviors. They look for people who can be steadfast without being stubborn and be determined as well as diplomatic. These interviewers ask questions that look for behaviors that prove an applicant can endure the friction of culture add without steamrolling over others. They pose follow-up questions that ask interviewees to exemplify those behaviors. Seeing past buzzwords like "grit," they ask candidates to provide specifics from their past to prove the desired behavior is a part of their work history.

Another technique is to create hypothetical scenarios that require applicants to imagine how they might demonstrate "culture add" behavior. When an interviewer asks about a person's past experiences with constructive dissent in their history, asking about hypotheticals can show whether those characteristics are likely to stay with them into the future. Social identity bias is often rooted in status quo bias. A way to get over both is to conduct interviews in ways that require all candidates to defy the status quo. To give a fair shot to candidates who are marginalized, organizations can ensure certain questions are centralized. Possibilities include the following:

- How would you change our company?
- What's wrong with our business?
- What problems do you anticipate for this industry?
- Review our organization's strategies, and identify three gaps that should be filled.
- How do you convince people to improve something we didn't think needed improving?
- How do you deal with people who resist advice even against their own self-interest?

For some organizations, it can be divisive to use social identity for deciding who advances beyond the interview stage. Nevertheless, studies show that people from underrepresented groups have a harder time doing so. Restructuring interview questions so all interviewees must give underrepresented perspectives offers some correction. For those scared or resistant to interviewing for diversity, there is always the ability to restructure the interviewing process by looking for and rewarding "culture add."

6. THINK CREATIVELY ABOUT ANONYMIZING INTERVIEWS.

Sociologist Devah Pager arranged a group of participants to interview for jobs that required no experience and only a high school education. The only difference between interviewees? Race and criminal record. In the end, she found that the callback rate of White applicants *with* a criminal record was 17 percent while the callback rate of Black applicants *without* a criminal record was only 14 percent.

In one of the most famous examples of this approach, symphony orchestras identified gender disparities. In 1970, female musicians made up 6 percent in the five highest-ranked orchestras in the US. Those who wanted greater gender diversity pinpointed auditions as a primary issue. Decision makers chose musicians based on auditions. Many argued that gender had nothing to do with the selection process. According to them, bias played no role in their evaluations, they picked the best musicians, and they shouldn't start modifying their process to consider identity.

Faced with the insistence that deciders should just focus on the music, some orchestras started focusing on the music even more. Responding to evaluators who claimed to be objective, they performed a kind of philosophical judo. If judges insisted they didn't consider the gender of performers when they made their decisions, then they wouldn't have to see the gender of any performers at all. Some had

performers audition through recordings. Others did so behind curtains. Some even went so far as to put down padding so evaluators
couldn't hear high heels.

Without data that could identify a musician's gender, judges chose
a higher percentage of female musicians. In their analysis of this
data, economists Claudia Goldin and Cecilia Rouse note that using a
screen for auditions "increases—by 50 percent—the probability that
a woman will be advanced from certain preliminary rounds and increases by several fold the likelihood that a woman will be selected in
the final round." They conclude that this "blind auditioning" dra-
matically increases impartiality at minimal cost, leading them to
conclude "that the adoption of the screen and blind auditions served
to help female musicians in their quest for orchestral positions."

Similarly, the virtues of these auditions can apply to other forms of
anonymized interviewing. Bias drives interviewers to assess the social
identity of the person sitting across the table. In addition to hearing
answers to questions, they might see data like ethnicity, gender, and
socioeconomic class that could prove irrelevant to a candidate's qualifications. Traditionalists who conduct conventional interviews insist
they just ignore these things, but studies like those covered above
show they do come into play. This research also suggests the virtues of
putting up metaphorical screens between auditioners and their audi-
tors. The same way many orchestras had musicians perform behind
curtains, anonymized interviews can do the same by giving interviewees a certain amount of time to submit written responses to questions.

Some hirers might assume interviews are essential to determine
the "real-time" and presumably more honest answers of respondents.
In these cases, use the digital chat functions that exist on many

platforms to get the synchronous responses some crave while maintaining the anonymity that circumvents interview bias. If this approach seems farfetched, others include hiring a third party from outside the organization to conduct interviews.

Whatever the approach, the results of screened auditions challenge interviewers to circumvent their biases by exploring creative ways to anonymize interviews by removing the interviewee. If, as critics of DEI say, the point of an interview is to narrow focus on the best person for the job, the point should become even narrower. Most interview scenarios focus on the best person sitting in the chair across from the interviewer. Perhaps there are other ways to ensure we hire the best mind for the job—the person who gives the best answers to interview questions regardless of where the interviewee happens to be sitting.

7. MAKE THE SELECTION PROCESS TRANSPARENT.

Organizational leadership professor Stefanie K. Johnson presses leaders who genuinely seek hiring diversity to develop a clearly articulated process. Gone are the days of resting on clichés like "culture fit," "most qualified," or "best person for the job." You must be able to define these categories and pinpoint evidence of them. Beyond being able to identify the criteria you use, you must be able to explain "*how* you are setting the criteria" in the first place. According to Johnson, the best way to create an inclusive culture is to create one that includes people in the decision-making process or at least helps them see what it looks like.

To this end, she advocates what she calls "aggressive transparency." According to her, "passive transparency is sharing the information for those who want to look. Aggressive transparency is *making* them look. . . . You create infographics, you tweet about it, you post on Instagram or on the company's intranet or put signs around the office." To defend against accusations of unfair hiring practices, leaders must be more transparent.

To achieve this level of openness, prepare a timeline of decisions and rationale. This is a sampling of the kinds of questions a transparent hirer would be prepared to answer.

1. When did the organization identify the need for the new position? Why?
2. How did the job description form?
3. Who formed it?
4. Was there a hiring committee? Why or why not?
5. Who was on it?
6. How was it decided who would be on it?
7. Who on the committee was responsible for what?
8. How was the job advertisement drafted and why?
9. Where was it posted and why?
10. Being as specific as possible, which criteria were used to identify the résumés that would receive callbacks?
11. What steps were made to manage the biases inherent in the résumé-review process?
12. Which criteria were used to identify which interviewees would advance?

13. How were interviews conducted?

14. Given all the ways bias can undermine the interview process, what steps were taken to remain fair?

15. How were interviewees assessed?

16. How was the final selection decided?

17. Who made the decision? How?

18. Why that person or those people?

In addition to these questions, take time to list others that would be valuable at your particular organization to be transparent and show that your hiring process was as inclusive as possible.

8. PROVIDE BETTER MESSAGING.

Social psychologist Adam D. Galinsky notes that many DEI advocates forget to message their programs effectively and end up harming the same communities they hope to serve. In "Maximizing the Gains and Minimizing the Pains of Diversity," he points out that some team members view opportunity as a zero-sum game. When DEI programs seem to give a bigger slice of the pie to an underrepresented group, others can feel they are losing a piece of it. The point is to let people know you aren't taking away a slice of that pie and giving it to someone else; you are growing the pie for everyone. As Galinsky claims, DEI programs become effective only insofar as "they are inclusive of all employees, benefiting minority groups without creating perceived exclusion of majority groups."

Resistance will arise if you're hiring a Black person just to hire a Black person, so you'll have to articulate what specific skills you want that candidate to have. Psychologists Wiebren S. Jansen, Sabine Otten, and Karen I. van der Zee study the effects of diversity approaches on majority members. They find that standard DEI initiatives usually happen between minority groups, HR, ERGs, DEI officers, and company leadership. When this approach leaves out majority members, they view inclusion efforts negatively. However, when those same initiatives involved majority members all along the process, the entire organization saw higher support and greater success. In short, Jansen, Otten, and van der Zee conclude that inclusion efforts should include everyone.

A key element of this inclusion is explaining the rationale behind diversity hiring. If it's expanding into the market of African American urban professionals ages thirty-five to fifty in the Midwest, then specify that you're looking for a candidate who has a deep understanding of how to reach that demographic. This is not synonymous with "reverse discrimination." It doesn't say that you're looking to hire only Black people. In fact, it leaves open the possibility that a White person could get the job, if they're the most qualified in this particular area. Remember that most people assume organizations should hire for "culture fit," so if you're hiring for "culture add," you must explain how diversity hiring will add to the entire company culture. If reaching African American urban professionals ages thirty-five to fifty in the Midwest will increase your company's market share by 8 percent and revenue by 14 percent, foreground these statistics.

Beyond providing high-level numbers, translate them into benefits for individuals. Will this increased market share lead to a 2 percent raise for every member of the team? Will this increased revenue help you hire three support staff members? How will hiring someone with expertise in this area improve efficiency, focus, and ease? Let team members know how a new position will benefit them. Articulate how hiring someone with expertise in and knowledge of underrepresented groups will help them.

Remember that some view diversity hiring as a philanthropic or political venture. They assume minority groups pressure employers to help the underprivileged in ways that damage the financial health of the company. If you work in an organization like this, be proactive. From the start, show how diversity hiring improves productivity, innovation, and retention for the entire organization. Return to chapter 3, where we made the financial and the moral case for DEI. Use that information to show how a specific job search conducted in a more inclusive way can translate into specific benefits for each individual.

Watching for "No-Brainers"

This chapter began with a story about how a board of well-intentioned people unknowingly let racial bias drive their hiring decisions. They never said they didn't want to hire Anitra because she was African American or wanted to hire Wendy because she was White. But they did use Eurocentric definitions of "executive presence" and socioeconomic affinity for a candidate who lived in their neighborhood to make those decisions. The social identity bias that made their applicant selection seem like a "no-brainer" shows the extent to which biases make decisions for us.

The problem lies with "no-brainers." When decisions seem obvious, self-evident, or straightforward, there is a series of assumptions at play that makes them seem that way. "No-brainers" don't provide transcendent insight into universal truths. They provide "good feelings," "culture fits," and status quo biases that continue to disadvantage underrepresented communities. They make applicants with White-sounding names more likely to receive a callback than counterparts with Black-sounding names. They make White interviewees with a criminal record more likely to receive a callback than Black applicants without one. They make Wendy more likely to get hired than Anitra for little more than the fact that she lives in the same neighborhood as her interviewers.

To avoid problems with hiring, the inclusive leader needs to guard against following their gut. As any data-driven organization knows, the gastrointestinal tract isn't a reliable compass. In a strange twist, for more evidence-based decision-making that is also more inclusive, sometimes the answer to avoiding problematic "no-brainers" is in narrowing the amount of data available to the brain.

CHAPTER SIX

Onboarding
"Look Who's Hanging
with the Boys!"

Once I secured my first internship, I threw myself headlong into the experience. Grateful for the chance to show what I could do, I decided to be the first to show up and the last to leave. I knew the organization was trying to bring in more diversity, and was glad that I was getting the opportunity to demonstrate the value that I could bring. In this high-stakes situation where so many were eager to watch these changes fail, I also knew I couldn't make a single mistake.

A few weeks into the program, however, I started noticing that other interns were advancing in ways I wasn't. They were getting more visible and valuable work assignments. They were working with more senior leaders than I was. Had I done something wrong? Had I offended certain power brokers or failed to perform? What kinds of hidden rituals had I violated to keep finding myself one step behind my peers in the job allocation process?

I went to my mentor with these questions. He ran down the usual list. "How are your relationships?" "Good, I know everyone on a first-name basis, and they all know me. I go out of my way to make personal connections and establish rapport." "What about meeting deadlines?" "Absolutely. Above and beyond punctual, running at breakneck speed to ensure the only deadline I'd miss was a reasonable bedtime." But then he asked, "How's happy hour?"

And I stopped in my tracks. Happy hour? It hadn't even crossed my mind. Noting my confusion, my mentor said that was the source of my problems. I hadn't offended anyone. I hadn't done anything wrong. It was that I had failed to join the group at the local watering hole. As naive as I was incredulous, I assumed my absence couldn't have been that big a deal. My career couldn't be endangered just because I'd neglected to think about frequenting a grimy bar, but my mentor said that was exactly the case. Determined to prove my dedication and despite my discomfort with bars, I resolved to take advantage of this professional opportunity.

During the next happy hour, as I walked toward the group from work, one of the male interns howled at me, "Look who's hanging with the boys!" Every eye turned toward me, the only woman in the place, standing in heels, skirt, and blouse, praying to all that was holy they wouldn't expect me to ride the mechanical bull.

In many ways, a fundamental problem with this story is a problem with onboarding. In the first months of a team member's employment, an organization should clarify expectations, articulate procedures, and work to make an environment where new hires want to stay. During all the orientation sessions I had during those initial weeks, no one ever stated that if an intern wanted to advance, they had to attend happy hour. To make matters worse, this social event was so central to the White men gathered in that bar they never even recognized it was something they needed to explain. Even if they had, they never wondered whether it was something they should be doing in the first place.

At the end of my internship, I declined the offer for a full-time position. When I shared this with my mentor, he said it was strange that an organization would do all that work to make their hiring process more inclusive only to drop the ball when it came to onboarding. But this story isn't extraordinary. In my work, I talk to countless people who've decided to leave their organizations within a few days, hours, even minutes because of something related to onboarding. For this reason, leaders who want to avoid losing time, money, and new hires need to do more than wait for people from underrepresented groups to start "hanging with the boys."

The Importance of Onboarding

For our purposes here, we'll define onboarding as anywhere between the first three months to the first year of an employee's work at an organization. It refers to the process that is designed to help new hires learn everything they need to join the team effectively. According to a Society for Human Resource Management report, a successful onboarding experience alone can improve performance up to 11 percent. In 2009, an Aberdeen Group survey found that 86 percent of respondents felt new hires decided whether to commit to a company within the first six months on the job.

Despite the importance of onboarding, professor of management Talya Bauer notes 30 percent of organizations engage in "passive onboarding." These companies concentrate on legal issues, formalities, and role clarification in an onboarding process that speeds through "a checklist of unrelated tasks to be completed."

This process becomes especially fraught when new hires are from demographics with a history of society violently forcing their entire group to assimilate. In the workplace, people from underrepresented groups can anticipate actions that disparage, stereotype, and minimize them. To avoid danger, minority members learn to practice hypervigilance, poring over statements, policies, and practices of an organization for signs of threat. Because social existence for marginalized people is one that is dangerous, a primary purpose of onboarding this group should be convincing them the organization is a place where they can feel safe.

Some don't think twice about distributing opportunities at a place that feels threatening to others. If the bar is full of drunk men riding mechanical bulls, this onboarding experience sends a message. It suggests that the organization doesn't care for the safety of a woman trying to avoid inebriated catcalls. What's worse, it says that the business never even considered this threat at all.

This disregard erodes morale, productivity, and creativity. According to Julia Rozovsky, director of people operations at Google, a prerequisite of innovation is psychological safety. In "The Five Keys to a Successful Google Team," she argues, "Psychological safety was far and away the most important of the five dynamics we found." Even an organization that prides itself on bold thinking must make extraordinary strides to convince newcomers that they will be allowed to think boldly. During the onboarding period, new hires take a defensive posture. They are working hard to fit in and retain their position. In short, once they're hired, new employees are eager to surrender the very differences that got them hired in the first place.

The onboarding process must dissuade them from this tendency by proving to new employees that they have room to experiment, fail, and disagree. In the end, people with higher psychological safety are less likely to leave; "they're more likely to harness the power of diverse ideas from their teammates, they bring in more revenue, and they're rated as effective twice as often by executives."

Despite the importance of creating the psychological safety that's essential for productivity, many organizations that have problems retaining people from marginalized backgrounds for longer than a few months come to me scratching their heads.

Steps for Inclusivity

1. CHANGE YOUR PHILOSOPHICAL APPROACH TO ONBOARDING.

When thinking about onboarding, reject the tendency to prioritize assimilation. Even better, go beyond inclusion that merely tolerates difference. If you want to increase retention and maximize profitability, restructure onboarding so it fosters difference. Instead of settling on "culture add," use those new hires' first few months to foster "culture change." The former approach prioritizes the individual's relationship to a rigid company, while the latter recognizes the extent to which a business hires individuals precisely because they want them to help the organization evolve. The purpose of onboarding should be to renegotiate an organization's identity in light of the new identities that join it. For example, Quora is noted for an onboarding process that is so focused on new hires that mentors budget 25 percent of personal output time to guide the initial weeks of training.

They structure this process so employees start working on manageable projects in their first week and work to help them articulate their goals.

Within the first few months, those who are recruited by a company for their underrepresented perspective can see whether they'll be ignored. Once that realization sets in, it takes the tokenized only a few seconds to fire off a post that can expose the company. In the age of social media and Glassdoor reviews, onboarding becomes the ultimate test of whether a company practices what it preaches. One bad onboarding experience undermines the ability of a business to onboard others. Those who assume marginalized people will figure out that they're supposed to drink with the boys soon find themselves wondering why all their diversity hiring has failed.

On the other hand, inclusive leaders recognize the onboarding process for what it is: a soft open that showcases their ability to host. The stakes are high, and the scrutiny is intense. But this kind of trial by fire can purify intentions and remove compromising alloys. Every onboarding session with underrepresented groups is a moment for an organization to hold itself up for examination. It is a moment to declare DEI objectives and ensure that the company is fulfilling them. It provides opportunities for an internal culture to rehearse who it is and wants to be for new team members.

According to Sarah Cordivano, associate director of global diversity, equity, and inclusion at Springer Nature, one value of inclusive onboarding is that it compels teams to put their principles into action, declaring them, explaining them, and showing them in concrete ways more frequently than they might in any other professional function. In addition to the internal fortification around DEI that the onboarding process provides, it is also an unparalleled opportunity to "build your brand externally because it shows your organization is a welcoming place where your employees feel safe to be their authentic selves."

2. CREATE AN ONBOARDING TEAM.

It will take some doing to start onboarding for culture change. To re-create your company culture in ways that allow underrepresented people to improve the organization, inclusive leaders examine their onboarding process. A key first step to this examination is to create an onboarding team. Rather than handing duties off to a single person reading from a binder or an informal network of coworkers who will teach newcomers the ropes as they go, active onboarders give this process the attention, care, and importance it deserves by assembling an entire committee of people to do the work.

3. ENSURE THE ONBOARDING TEAM IS DIVERSE.

According to chief diversity strategist of Rework Work, Stacey A. Gordon, the companies that see the greatest success with diversity hiring are those that follow it up with diverse onboarding teams. Giving new hires access to multiple people from different cultural backgrounds increases the likelihood that they will connect with the company's culture.

This group can also help make programming decisions for orientation events, initial training, and first-day events. A Muslim member of the committee could be the one who ends up reminding the team that they shouldn't take candidates to their first lunch at a rib shack. A person with vision loss might remind the team to ensure that all presentations are available through multiple senses for all levels of accessibility. A woman of color might point out that there must be a more inclusive way to distribute job assignments than at a mechanical bull-riding tournament. The problem with unconscious bias is that it remains unconscious, so it's important to get different kinds of consciousnesses working on an issue to mitigate all kinds of exclusionary assumptions.

4. SEND THE ONBOARDING TEAM THROUGH DEI TRAINING.

Just because an onboarder has the same ethnic identity as a new hire doesn't mean the former might not stumble into all kinds of ageist microaggressions that alienate the latter. Just because a senior partner at the law firm comes from the same working-class background as the law student doesn't mean they can't say the transphobic statements that drive the promising summer intern to a rival firm. Membership in one underrepresented group doesn't mean an automatic understanding of how to be inclusive for all.

For this reason, put the team through inclusion training that covers issues like privilege, bias, and microaggression. Beyond this more formal learning, it would also be valuable for the group to hold meetings to determine onboarding goals, DEI values, and possible complications. Before hosting new hires from marginalized communities, the group of hosts should have a strong understanding of shared terms, goals, and tactics. To achieve this, send your onboarding team through DEI training.

5. REVIEW ONBOARDING PAPERWORK.

Some DEI advocates rush through documents like the employee handbook, benefits packages, and the organization's expectations. For them, there's a difference between this technical information and the work of inclusion. But don't take for granted the part of the onboarding process where you cover the seemingly dry documents. The same way bias and privilege kept my fellow interns and leaders from thinking there was anything problematic about handing out assignments during happy hour, overfamiliarity with these mundane documents can keep you from recognizing problems that can exist with them.

For example, if the job advertisement proclaims that the organization believes in the virtues of DEI, ensure the handbook has a DEI statement and policy. If the company spent much of the hiring process bragging about how much it values inclusion, make sure pre-onboarding literature contains clear definitions and expectations regarding it. Many businesses talk enough about diversity to hire diverse talent and then end up seeming like performative allies when they fail to mention diversity once in the documents that dictate the terms and conditions of employment.

In addition to stating your DEI values, chart your processes. Part of proving your dedication to diversity is to show people how to pursue legal action if that dedication is violated. Have an anti-discrimination statement and policy as well as a clearly articulated discrimination report process. Beyond these items, look for other ways to review onboarding paperwork so DEI becomes a more central part of it.

6. INCLUDE ALL IDENTITY OPTIONS.

If an employee has changed their name from the one that appears on official documents, allow them the option to change it. If names have characters like accent marks, umlauts, cedillas, and tildes, double-check that online questionnaire software can accept, retain, and reprint those accents. Many people identify with multiple racial and ethnic identities, so your reporting data should permit that option. Ensure your forms go beyond "M/F" to include all gender identities.

In fact, for all these examples as well as those I haven't listed, move beyond software that requires people to choose from a list of provided options. Update to formats that allow respondents to fill in blanks. To some, making these little changes can seem insignificant, but these alterations can have a profound impact. There are many who are used to completing innumerable forms that ignore their identities. For them, these changes can mark one of the first instances that recognize their whole selves.

7. CONSIDER COMMUNITY CONNECTIONS.

Remember that a member of an underrepresented group isn't just underrepresented in the workplace. They are often underrepresented in the larger society as well. If you have an analyst moving from Peru to Wisconsin, they might be the only immigrant, Peruvian, or Spanish speaker in the company. The culture shock that can come from this realization might be exacerbated by the fact that they've also moved to a climate that's significantly colder. Like the chill of winter, a person's nationality, ethnicity, or language doesn't end when they exit the company doors. For this reason, pre-onboarding teams should explore options for community connections. In this example, a leader could create a welcome package with gift certificates to a nearby Peruvian restaurant or tickets to a concert at a South American community center. Be creative. Beyond selling your company, remember you're also selling your city. Show members from marginalized groups that there are opportunities in your geographical area where they can find support.

8. CREATE A PRE-ONBOARDING STAGE.

According to applied social psychologist Jamie A. Gruman and professor of organizational behavior and HR management Alan M. Saks, best practices for bringing in new employees include taking all the compliance items many use during the first few days of work and shifting them to asynchronous activities before orientation even begins. The sea of forms to sign, presentations to hear, and handbook issues to cover—many of the checklist items passive onboarders assume constitute the entire onboarding process—can be finished with a few emails, prerecorded videos, or postage stamps. Pre-onboarding helps new hires process overwhelming information at their own pace and in the privacy of their own homes instead of under time constraints. In fact, one study found that creating a pre-onboarding process that is separate from the onboarding process can improve the retention rates of first-year hires by 81 percent.

According to HR business partner Kaitlyn Pavlina, pre-boarding "allows the first day to be focused around welcoming the new hire into the organization and the rest of the first week to focus on education and socialization." Have meet and greets, lunches, scheduled coffees, and check-ins. Instead of tricking hires into a room just to bombard them with fresh information, share homework so they can catch up to speed and feel like they're part of the process. Give them indications about what to expect during those initial days. Provide specific questions for discussion and particular areas of data to explore. Share enough information so new hires can get involved. If you want to raise the profile of overlooked voices, start before their first day even begins by giving them all the resources they need to discuss matters on a level playing field.

9. INVOLVE NEW HIRES IN PLANNING THEIR WELCOMING ACTIVITIES.

Avoid assuming strategies that work for majority members will work for minority members. At the same time, don't make assumptions about what people from underrepresented groups want. Don't assume all Black men want to go to a soul food restaurant. Plenty prefer vegan food. Don't assume all Black women want a list of salons as part of their welcome package. Avoid prejudice, bias, and assumptions about what people want by simply asking them. If you want to retain the surprise that comes from welcoming activities and don't want to explicitly ask people to structure their own first few days, create a few inconspicuous and informal conversations. Use these seemingly unrelated and fun "get-to-know-me" exercises to plan the kinds of surprise activities you'll structure. Besides, if the point of all this planning is to make people feel included, you should include them in that actual planning.

10. INCLUDE DIVERSE PERSPECTIVES.

Andy Przystanski, senior content marketing manager at Lattice, says that the main point of onboarding should help new people gauge an organization's ability to foster belonging. According to him, because recruits are "trying to picture themselves succeeding at the company, your training lineup matters." For people from underrepresented groups, an important part of picturing themselves in the organization can be seeing their social identities represented in the presenters. He notes, "If someone new comes into your business and every single person that trains them or that they meet is white, straight, and predominantly men, that won't give off the best impression." If you want to retain diverse hires, make sure your onboarding has people from diverse backgrounds.

11. INVITE ERG LEADERS.

Despite the value of including diverse perspectives, there are better approaches than just grabbing the nearest Black guy and having him talk about what it's like to work in a predominantly White institution. Beyond parading out a lineup of BIPOC, women, and LGBTQ+ to prove you have a diverse cast, have speakers who lead ERGs. Employee resource groups, business resource groups, or affinity groups provide a community for team members within an organization that share a social identity. Having leaders from ERGs speak during your onboarding process is beneficial for a few reasons.

For starters, it shows the organization goes beyond including individual minorities to create groups that support those populations.

Second, it avoids the false assumption that people from under-represented groups have the time, energy, desire, or ability to talk about social identity with others. However, if you ask ERG leaders to do the same thing, the situation changes. By leading the group, they are implicitly saying that they want to talk about social identity and its relationship to the workplace. The fact that they belong to this kind of group suggests they are willing to work with other employees, especially new ones, so they can thrive in the organization.

Third, ERG leaders can go beyond talking about identity to invite new hires to join a community. They can go beyond describing what it's like to be a woman working at the organization and detail what activities the women's ERG has for the next year. Beyond reflecting who new hires are, ERG leaders can advertise things they can do.

12. DECLARE YOUR COMMITMENT TO DEI.

Don't assume being polite will be enough to foster a sense of inclusion. Don't ignore difference by sweeping it under broad categories like kindness, respect, and fairness. Values statements with opaque words like these ring hollow. The presence of these broad words can suggest an organization hasn't considered the specifics of problems like workplace racism, sexism, homophobia, transphobia, xenophobia, or ableism.

To prove you are a place dedicated to inclusion, you must state so. Provide specifics. With plans, procedures, and policies, you must prove you're as inclusive as you claim to be. Talk about your goals and share your accomplishments. Note climate surveys and demographic statistics, even unflattering ones. Many employers use diversity, equity, inclusion, belonging, justice, and accessibility as empty buzzwords. Prove your authentic commitment by foregrounding your DEI journey. Have the courage to state objectives. Have the bravery to admit failures. Improve the onboarding process with these acts of good faith.

13. ASK FOR FEEDBACK.

Remember, the first few months of a team member's employment are crucial. They can be the deciding factor that determines whether all your recruiting and hiring efforts have been successful. They can be the point that makes or breaks your entire DEI strategy, so get data. Don't wait for exit interviews once team members have already decided to terminate their relationship with the company. Don't seek insights only after something goes wrong. Seek feedback at multiple stages of the process.

End orientation day with a questionnaire. Conclude the first week with another. Do the same after the first month and quarter. Take steps to highlight inquiries that specifically address issues related to DEI. Move beyond asking how well the individual is fitting in to asking tougher questions regarding how the organization can do a better job to make all people feel welcome.

To encourage honesty, make the surveys anonymous. If the number of people going through the onboarding process is so small a number it might undermine this confidentiality, use a third party. Invite a peer, consultant, HR rep, or colleague from another company to sit in on the process and provide feedback. Whatever you do, improve onboarding by seeking feedback.

14. USE FEEDBACK TO HELP THE ORGANIZATION EVOLVE.

Every year, organizations spend fortunes on consultants. In this capacity, they pay outsiders for their unvarnished perspectives of the company. Of course, these advisers have expertise in their areas. At the same time, however, if the point is to seek outside perspectives for a business's inner workings, onboarding can become a valuable two-way process. Some use it to force newcomers to conform. Others use it to preserve diversity and difference.

The most inclusive leaders, however, see the onboarding process as a unique chance to bring in fresh perspectives regarding how to change the organization. Companies that want the benefits of under-represented groups are also those willing to change based on their insights. Frequently, organizations use onboarding to show newcomers how they've always done things, but it can also be the place where newcomers show organizations how to improve things.

"Change with the Times"

This kind of inverted onboarding might not work for some organizations, but I suspect it would work for more than we'd admit. Inclusive leaders will spend serious time grappling with the possibilities this model presents. Even if it doesn't mean handing over the agenda to new hires, there are profound opportunities for those who put in the work. Some organizations see the first day, week, or quarter as the time to teach individuals the old ways. But there is room for individuals to teach organizations some fresh thinking. Again, if the point of DEI is to create the equitable structures and inclusive practices that make for diverse perspectives, what better way to prove it than by using those initial contacts to hear, celebrate, and promote a newcomer's ideas before they've had time to conform? Some of the above recommendations will work for your situation. Others might not. Use what works. Don't use what doesn't. But whatever you do, make the onboarding process more inclusive by ensuring it doesn't compel newcomers to "hang with the boys" as much as it challenges your organization to "change with the times."

CHAPTER SEVEN

Retention
From Poaching to Coaching

A few months after I started working for a company I'll call Acme, a multibillion-dollar international firm, I approached company leaders with a plan to start a social entrepreneurship wing for their organization. I presented a strategy to both profit on their investments and support social good. Before long, executives gave me a promotion.

But the joys of that advancement were quickly dashed when my direct manager, whom I'll refer to as Ryan, called me into his office. He echoed the praise of his peers and congratulated me on all we'd achieved. But then Ryan cleared his throat, leaned in, and warned that I shouldn't get too excited. While I hadn't asked for a promotion or even thought about setting my eyes on a corner office, he took it upon himself to let me know that Acme didn't promote minorities.

Ryan assured me they weren't "racist or anything like that." They invited hard work from any qualified employee. Nevertheless, they were cautious about promoting people of color too quickly for fear that "they'd get poached."

By the end of that afternoon, I circulated applications. By the end of that week, I already had a callback. By the end of that month, I had my first interview for the job that I would take. The new position gave me infinitely more freedom, a treasure trove of new connections, and almost one hundred times the budget.

This story isn't extraordinary. Too often, marginalized people feel tricked into a position only to end up serving as window dressing. They read the job advertisement with its pronouncements about being an EEO/AA employer, hear interviewers proclaim their dedication to equity, and even experience the first few months of an onboarding process that promises inclusion. After a while, however, the requests begin to pile up: start the ERG without compensation, facilitate a courageous conversation without resources, or attend a job fair for BIPOC college seniors without release time. Even if they don't find themselves Photoshopped into every piece of company publicity, many can feel invited through the door to be seen through the windows but kept in the lobby.

The leaders at Acme thought they were being inclusive because they promoted BIPOC. But their retention strategy also meant sabotaging the careers of those people, making sure not to promote them too fast because competitors might steal them away. Like Acme, many companies assume hiring someone, paying them, and making sure they don't suffer microaggressions should be enough to retain diverse talent. Then they're shocked when those populations leave to work someplace else. These leaders focus so much energy on making sure that a competitor doesn't "poach" diverse hires, that they forget to invest energy in making sure that they coach them.

If you want to retain the marginalized members of your team, you must make a retention plan. Study after study shows that traditional methods benefit traditional candidates and end up losing nontraditional hires. If you want to improve retention among new populations, you must practice some new retention practices.

The Importance of Retention

Most organizations were never built with marginalized people in mind. Even those that strive to be inclusive will inherit the assumptions of a business culture that is homogeneous. One of the most pervasive assumptions is that there is a clear division between the personal and the professional. Some long for the good old days when work was work, people did their job, collected a check, and went home. Some imagine a time before everyone brought the messiness of their personal lives into the workplace. But drawing up arbitrary divisions between the professional, personal, and social in ways that might not apply to people from underrepresented groups can be an outdated and expensive view.

In "Companies Need to Know the Dollar Cost of Employee Turnover," *Forbes* senior contributor Bill Conerly notes turning over an entry-level position costs 50 percent of that salary, midlevel is 125 percent, and senior executive is 200 percent. Beyond the direct costs associated with replacing one position, there are other drains on productivity. If one person leaves a position, it can inspire others to do the same. Even if remaining team members want to stay, the loss of one from their ranks increases the workload for all, and that added stress can be the thing that sends even an enthusiastic worker out the door.

Whenever a worker leaves, they take immeasurable amounts of institutional knowledge with them, everything from the most efficient way to file that report or the reminders to renew snow removal con-tracts. Even the smoothest departures cause friction. Even the best replacements need time before they can operate at full capacity, and require attention away from those already working at full capacity to explain procedures. Lower productivity and higher supervision ex-penses lead Conerly to conclude no rational leader can "cheap-shot employee retention efforts when they have seen the real dollars and cents costs of employee turnover."

These costs are even more serious when it comes to retaining di-verse employees. Acme, the company that appeared in the story that started this chapter, had a retention problem. Long before I left the organization to help start another, leaders complained about the fact that Black workers didn't stay. When a marginalized person would leave, executives kept blaming the employee for being too undisci-plined, sensitive, or lazy to hack it. Without asking what structural issues might have led to one Black person's departure, they would replace one with another. Then, after a short time, that replacement would leave only to be replaced by another who would stay for a few months before leaving, and so on.

In this regard, my previous employer wasn't extraordinary. Nu-merous organizations have a retention problem with underrepre-sented people. Some leaders blame the workers who leave, but the best look inward. They examine themselves and see how the compa-ny's poor retention practices may be to blame for departures. While this process is uncomfortable, it is important. Organizations cannot ignore the costs of failing to retain diverse talent. Conversely, they cannot overlook the fact that if they learn how to retain the most marginalized of their members, they will end up benefiting everyone.

Steps for Inclusivity

1. INTERROGATE YOUR RETENTION PLAN.

During diversity audits, I'll ask clients what their plan is for retaining team members. Most shrug and say they've never articulated one. But not having a plan is a plan. Taking a passive approach to retention implies that you assume retention is a given. If you do nothing, you presume you don't have to do anything. What other business relationship could survive with this approach? How long would customers remain loyal if you stopped marketing to them, improving your product according to their requests, or listening to them at all? How long would you have an important client if you never held meetings, reassessed the relationship, or even checked in?

Business is a responsive sector, willing to transform itself and evolve to change according to what customers, consumers, and clients want or what competitors, currencies, or economies do. Yet, when it comes to relationships with team members, leaders can become surprisingly clueless. If a paycheck constitutes your entire retention plan, you will attract employees who require little but also tend to give less.

Conversely, if you ignore those who expect more but give the most, you'll lose them to the industry rivals that are willing to give even the minimal attention necessary to reap maximum gains. If you haven't actively articulated a retention plan, you've passively inherited one. If you haven't intentionally designed one to be inclusive, you've unintentionally reinforced one that is exclusive.

If you don't take the time to orchestrate new strategies to make your workplace one where BIPOC, women, LGBTQ+, people with disabilities, and veterans want to stay, you're resting on old ones that never gave them a second thought. For this reason, why would any-one want to stay with your organization? What does it do to encourage them to stay? What does it offer that others don't?

2. DEVELOP A FORMAL RETENTION PLAN.

Most organizations already have "exit interviews" that seek insights from employees on their way out, but what about introducing formalized check-ins while they're still coming through the door? Instead of waiting until separation, touch base before problems arise. For this, conduct "stay interviews" that focus on the needs of employees and ways the organizations can continuously improve when it comes to meeting those needs. Instead of assuming no news is good news, check in. At the same time, instead of letting your fears drive you to imagine the worst, touch base. Richard P. Finnegan, CEO of C-Suite Analytics and the Finnegan Institute and expert on stay interviews, recommends asking the following five questions:

1. What do you look forward to each day when you commute to work (or log in to your virtual office, for people who work from home)?
2. What are you learning here, and what do you want to learn?
3. Why do you stay here?
4. When is the last time you thought about leaving us, and what prompted it?
5. What can I do to make your job better for you?

Diversity audits, climate surveys, and pay equity investigations have their place, but also make sure you talk to your underrepresented team members. Releasing inclusion statements is important, but make sure to also include the marginalized by meeting face-to-face with them. Think about stay interviews as reverse interviews. During the hiring interview, you asked candidates all questions they had to answer in order to work for the organization. Think of these reverse interviews as opportunities for you to ask team members to determine what the organization must do to keep them working for *it*. Making this shift improves retention and morale and lets employees know you are serious about creating a better workplace for them.

In addition to these stay interviews, improve your exit interviews. When diverse employees have decided to leave the company, they can provide "real, unvarnished insight into how companies can better serve underrepresented employees." Give these exit interviews and their participants the same amount of attention and respect you would extend to a high-cost consultant for the same information.

3. PROVIDE INCLUSIVITY TRAINING.

The same way you shouldn't assume your retention plan is inclusive if you haven't intentionally made it so, don't assume your team is naturally inclusive if they haven't strategically learned how to become so. It's tempting to focus DEI training on people managers, but broaden your view. To demonstrate a commitment to DEI, team members need to hear senior leaders talking the talk and walking the walk. At the same time, all the leaders from the CEO down to a direct supervisor can know all the things to foster belonging, but a steady barrage of microaggressions from entry-level peers can be the thing that causes minority members to head for the door.

For these reasons, make training available to everyone. Use these sessions as opportunities to articulate how DEI benefits all the members of the organization, not just the underrepresented. Create a common language, and rehearse the company's values. Show people how to be inclusive, and remind them why it matters. Focus on productive, solutions-based, and practical lessons that help participants see the value of being inclusive.

Companies can benefit when team members from any background feel they are a part of the organization. To foster connection, everyone must feel safe to contribute. Only once a leader achieves this measure can they earn the credibility that fosters even higher engagement. People can resent being asked for their input only to have those insights shot down. The tendency to dismiss contributions becomes even more problematic among team members from marginalized communities that have historical, social, and political experiences of being ignored.

According to Ian Heinig of The Manifest, how well an organization includes people from underrepresented social groups becomes a barometer for how well it can retain people from other populations. In a survey of 540 full-time employees, he found 79 percent "will not accept a job with a higher salary from a company that failed to act against employees who were involved in sexual harassment." Seventy-one percent of respondents also found it intolerable to work for a company that pays female and minority employees less than others. According to this data, inclusive strategies designed to retain diverse individuals prove a commitment to doing what is right. The added benefit of also retaining other populations comes from being equitable.

Rather than forcing fearful or guilt-ridden compliance, foster enthusiastic support for DEI. Regular training can minimize conflict and show diverse employees that you stand with them. Beyond group training, consider more-personalized outside consultation. Consider individual coaching for yourself, key leaders, or resistant members of the team. There are many educational situations that are high stakes because of either how powerful the person is or how problematic they might be. For these, private opportunities can permit the honesty, growth, and transformative learning necessary for the most impact.

4. REVISE RULES TO BE MORE INCLUSIVE.

Investigate employee handbooks, codes of conduct, and HR policies. Look for things that penalize culturally relative behavior or confuse the values of one social identity for the morals that should govern all social identities. Beware of dress codes that claim to maintain professionalism. Many have more restrictions on what women wear than men, suggesting they're interested in policing women's clothing more than promoting office standards. Watch out for policies regarding jewelry, clothing, and hairstyles that tend to punish people of color in ways that seem to take the culturally relative way many White people happen to dress and moralize it as the universal way all "respectable" people should dress. Review the Green Rabbits Graph you made in chapter 2. Examine all the professional biases you listed there. Use those as a springboard to interrogate the rules articulated by your onboarding materials.

Promote inclusive language and an inclusive approach to which languages one speaks. Provide options for people seeking gender-neutral or private restrooms as well as break-room options for people who need to breast pump or to work while watching children.

Whatever you do, if you want to retain a wider range of team members, remove policies that unnecessarily restrict who a person can be, and add other structures that support different ways of being.

5. USE FLEXIBLE SCHEDULING.

If you want innovative ideas, you'll have to accommodate people who have life situations that don't conform to conventional schedules. Being able to work in an office nine to five Monday through Friday privileges social groups who value compartmentalization in ways that separate the professional from the personal. It also restricts you to workers who have the socioeconomic and logistical support to facilitate the childcare, healthcare, and transportation required to block off forty hours of uninterrupted work. Conversely, innovative ideas come from thinking differently, which often comes with living differently. For example, a first-generation professional who can't drive to the office because their car's broken down can have an industry-altering revelation while working at two in the morning from their bedroom.

The US Department of Labor encourages leaders to explore flexible work arrangements. These looser structures allow room for "Customized Employment" that creates "flexibility around the job tasks rather than the location or the schedule." Structuring work around projects rather than time or place opens the labor market to a wide range of people with disabilities. It also benefits many veterans who have physical disabilities or mental health statuses that require more elastic scheduling.

According to the National Council on Disability, "The movement for flexibility in the workplace brings people with disabilities to . . . the discussion in which the workplace needs of all employees are taken into account." In "Building an Inclusive Workplace: Six Ways to Retain Diverse Talent," recruiter Abby Engers notes that this wider population includes "employees on maternity, family, medical, or disability leave."

Redefining work in these ways benefits individuals in these categories, but it also benefits organizations. As Engers points out, "Flexible schedules also reduce absenteeism, improve employees' health, and increase the retention of productive employees. Employees who have even a small degree of flexibility in when and where work got done also had significantly greater job satisfaction, stronger commitment to the job, and higher levels of engagement with the company, as well as significantly lower levels of stress."

Deloitte & Touche credits flexible work arrangements with retaining employees and saving $41.5 million in employee turnover costs. According to retention consultant Pam Lassiter, 70 percent of managers and 87 percent of employees "reported that having a flexible work arrangement made a positive or very positive impact on their productivity." If you want to improve retention, especially with underrepresented groups, explore ways your organization can implement flexible scheduling.

6. CREATE EMPLOYEE RESOURCE GROUPS.

ERGs are voluntary, employee-led groups whose aim is to foster a diverse, inclusive workplace aligned with the organizations they serve. These groups can offer places for people to connect with others who might share experiences. A women's group can provide advice to a woman who finds herself alone on a team. The monthly meeting of African American employees can offer understanding to a Black recruit who's just moved to town.

Beyond giving support to individuals, ERGs can amplify the voices of an entire group. A company might habitually misgender a transgender employee. That one person might raise objections, and the organization might ignore them. However, the multiple voices of an LGBTQ+ ERG can have a greater chance of encouraging the organization to take a more inclusive approach to pronouns.

Even for organizations that already make the lone woman, the new Black recruit, and the trans person feel included, having an ERG makes the structural commitment to inclusion. The presence of an affinity group can be a powerful first step in showing employees that leadership is willing to be held accountable. Having an entire group dedicated to the concerns of a marginalized community can prove that the organization is committed to hearing the concerns of that community.

Of course, the mere existence of these groups isn't enough. To encourage retention, leaders must give ERGs the funding, staffing, and resources that show they are valued. Create messaging to the entire organization that publicizes the groups, foregrounds upcoming events, and reminds people about the value of ERGs. Most important, train direct supervisors regarding the importance of giving team members time to attend ERG meetings.

Create opportunities for non-ERG members including and, perhaps especially, leaders to attend select ERG meetings. If a White leader attends the Latinx group or a self-identified Christian attends a meeting of Muslim employees to hear their concerns, these moments send the message that the company not only supports ERGs to help underrepresented people through the workplace, but also listens to those groups to help the entire organization improve that workplace.

7. STRUCTURE POSITIVE EXPERIENCES.

Many approaches to DEI concentrate on formal programs meant to solve problems. They focus on training designed to stop privilege, bias, and microaggressions. But these problem-solving approaches don't capture the entire picture. You can rid your organization of these problems and still not have diversity, equity, and inclusion because the absence of problems doesn't mean the presence of belonging.

In their paper "Deprivation at Work: Positive Workplace Experiences and the Racial Gap in Quit Intentions," Peter Norlander, Serena Does, and Margaret Shih note most organizational scholarship focuses on the negatives that actively harm performance when research must also address the absence of positives that passively do the same. For example, most DEI practitioners examine how the presence of active and large-scale discrimination drives minorities to quit, but they must also explore how passive and small-scale deprivations press marginalized communities to leave their jobs.

In two separate studies of nearly twenty-eight thousand people across the United States, Norlander, Does, and Shih found that workers of color experience more negative workplace experiences than their White counterparts. But the surprising fact was how frequently and deeply BIPOC felt this experience, not in terms of discrimination, but in deprivation. Results revealed marginalized people were 10 to 15 percent more likely to quit not because of enduring negative work experiences but because of "missing out on positive work experiences."

Most attention goes to how discriminatory hiring, promotion, and pay drive the underrepresented away, but this study found that small things like not getting invited to lunch, being excluded from water cooler conversations, or feeling disconnected from colleagues on a personal level influenced their quit intentions.

Many leaders approach inclusion like a Hippocratic oath to do no harm, but they must go further to also do good. This research encourages leaders to take a positive organizational approach so both managers and scholars "can benefit from efforts to move from a framework focused on curing illness to one focused on promoting health."

With these findings, inclusive leaders can improve retention by hosting. Throwing a party for mixed company doesn't just require you to remove fire hazards, clean mold, and ensure the food is sanitary. Removing dangers isn't the standard for good hosting; it's the bare minimum. You must also provide icebreakers, activities, and introductions.

Similarly, when creating an inclusive environment, it's not enough to set down a list of rules, training, and procedures that remove dangers. That's the minimum. You must also create opportunities for informal connections to happen. Don't wait for them to happen organically. No matter what kinds of inclusive measures you might establish in the workplace, your team members still have an entire social experience outside of that space. You might break down barriers by recruiting and hiring underrepresented people, but your team members will still have psychological barriers that encourage them to gravitate toward people like them. It's important to institute anti-discrimination policies, but you must also give people a reason to mingle.

Conclude meetings by taking turns for people to share things about themselves. Create a voluntary pool where participants get randomly grouped to have rotating coffee chats. While you might have to make sweeping changes to make your business more inclusive, remember that many of your team members will also have to make deep changes to their thinking.

For most, it's not common for them to connect with people who are different from them. For some, your new hire might be the first Hmong, gay, or disabled person they've ever met. Create fun and simple reasons to help them get over their habits and create the kinds of interpersonal micro-inclusions that are vital to overcoming deprivation and improving retention.

8. SUPPORT DEVELOPMENT.

According to a 2018 Gallup poll, "millennials fundamentally think about jobs as opportunities to learn and grow." Previous generations lived more compartmentalized lives, seeing other social institutions as a place for growth and seeing work as little more than a place for drudgery. While younger generations tend to expect more of their work, they also tend to give more. They seek development more than all other generations, and this desire for development makes them more likely to go above and beyond the call of mere responsibility.

In 2018, LinkedIn surveyed four thousand people and found 94 percent of employees would stay longer at an organization if it supported their development. At the same time, many respondents went on to say that a key to this learning was having the time to learn. Given these findings, a key element to retaining employees is giving them either the money or time for professional development.

Take a few minutes to consider how your organization could provide this support.

1. How much does your organization have budgeted for development?
2. If money is tight, where can your organization secure free training or allot time for people to learn on their own?
3. What kind of programming can you arrange so experts within your organization can train others, giving some an opportunity to display their knowledge and others the chance to learn?
4. How might your organization restructure performance reviews and promotion procedures to reward people for their professional development?

Whatever your answers to these questions, be creative about brainstorming ways to improve retention by supporting employee development.

9. PROVIDE A CLEAR PATH TO ADVANCEMENT.

History gives underrepresented people reason to be suspicious of the professional world. With the legacy of discrimination, they are justified in believing that the odds will be stacked against them. Even if recruiting, hiring, and onboarding defy these fears, many find their careers stalling. Even if a business removes obstacles to professional growth, they must articulate the path for advancement.

A Catalyst study found that the top three reasons why senior-level women leave a company are all related to progress. Forty-two percent sought increased compensation, 35 percent skills development, and 33 percent greater advancement. Whether for more money, skills, or opportunities, diverse populations leave an organization when they suspect it will hold them in place. Once again, we return to a primary threat for minority professionals: the trap of tokenism that lets people in the door but keeps them in the lobby.

To make matters worse, many of these respondents would consider staying if their employers were just more transparent. Many said they didn't even want advancement as much as a mere explanation of how to achieve it. Informal networks that are available to other populations help majority members develop an unspoken understanding of how to work their way up the ranks. If you belong to a group that just recently got access to the ladder, you might not know how to climb it.

For these reasons, Diversity Best Practices recommends that inclusive leaders "define and communicate clearly the criteria, process and expectations for upward mobility."

10. RETAIN LIKE YOU'RE COMPETING . . . BECAUSE YOU ALREADY ARE!

Focusing on the obstacles that impede advancement for underrepresented people, many overlook the practices that can also accelerate their progress. When leaders talk about how hard it is to retain marginalized groups, they assume there are organizational problems that drive these workers away. While this self-critique is valuable, it can also be narcissistic. Companies fail to retain minority members because of deficiencies in the organization, but they might also fail to retain them because other companies can attract them.

Retention is an issue between one organization and the individual worker, but it is also an issue among organizations. Sometimes the problem is with you, but sometimes the solutions are with someone else. Fifty-seven percent of employees want more diversity, 69 percent of executives think diversity and inclusion are the most critical issues, and 78 percent of people think DEI makes an organization more competitive. With statistics like these, leaders must go beyond assuming the status quo is enough to retain underrepresented people. They must also go beyond presuming that ridding their office of exclusion is enough. With most leaders identifying DEI as a top priority, simply being inclusive isn't enough. You must be *more* inclusive than the next organization.

Circle back to the Hampten Institute example from chapter 4. Identify all the things your organization would do to recruit people from that fictional school. Consider which are appropriate for retaining people from actual underrepresented groups. Identify ways to turn these plans into concrete action, realizing many of your competitors are already doing so.

The second I discovered identity-based obstacles at Acme, I found another place without them and moved on. Beyond circumventing both discrimination and deprivation, you must also recognize retention is a competition. For all its problems, the Acme company at the beginning of this chapter is still further along than many regarding DEI. At least Ryan recognized that people from marginalized communities were a valuable resource. He realized that, more than being a charity case he should accommodate, they were a coveted group that would get "poached." The underrepresented bring unique perspectives, experiences, and thinking that drive innovation, productivity, and profitability. So if you have a retention problem, it might be that your competitors recognize this fact better than you do.

To Stop Poaching, Start Coaching

While these strategies concentrate on retaining people from underrepresented groups, most improve retention of all employees. For example, if you adopt flexible work to improve conditions for people with disabilities, you can also retain and engage an employee who takes care of their aging parents. Some might resist these strategies, claiming they favor particular social groups. To earn support for these proposals, show how retaining those most likely to leave the organization benefits everyone. Point out that voluntary turnover costs US businesses $1 trillion every year. Explain that retaining employees means higher pay, greater benefits, and workplace stability for everyone. Note that improving life for those who might leave improves life for all who stay.

To improve retention, your plan must be more than simply to

retain. In fact, the best way to retain underrepresented people is to stop using the word "retention" altogether. The goal isn't to keep them; the goal is to grow them. Move beyond simply creating structures to maximize productivity for you and begin making opportunities for people to realize their full potential.

I would have stayed at Acme if they had given me room for growth. Once it became clear they wouldn't, it didn't take long before I found another organization that would. Because that second organization gave me opportunities, I gave them my all, and we grew in ways that surpassed anything Acme has ever done since. But the strange thing is that if Acme had given me support as though they were trying to advance me, that probably would have been precisely the thing to keep me there. In a strange paradox, other inclusive leaders find the same. Oftentimes, all you need to stop poaching is to start coaching.

CHAPTER EIGHT

Mentoring
Share the View

I t had been eight months since I joined a company I'll call Generic Corp. and basically created my position. I advocated for resources and articulated a plan to figure out ways to balance what the company had always done with something it had never done. Senior leadership was pleased with the results. Costs were low and results were impressive. We'd raised the profile of the business and ventured into new areas all while minimizing risks. Bringing my experience from working with much leaner organizations, I was able to build using a fraction of the cost. Because of this fiscal responsibility, leaders were even ready to fund the initiatives that were sure to benefit the community even more.

And that's when I received an email from Tom. He was a veritable force at Generic Corp., the heir apparent positioned for the CEO position, known for his ambition, efficiency, and brutal honesty. Seeing the name of his assistant in my inbox alongside one of those ominous "high-importance" exclamation points felt like a bucket of ice water poured down my throat. I rode the elevator up to the executive office. I stood in the office and saw the wall of windows that overlooked the city, a view of the skyline that seemed to stretch on forever.

"You're obviously hardworking, smart, and promising," Tom said. "You've done amazing things in such a short amount of time." I thanked him cautiously, still waiting for the other shoe to drop, when it finally came. "You should be far ahead of where you already are, but I don't know if it's in the cards." He went on to explain that while he knew I'd brought value to Generic, other key decision makers didn't. The problem was that I'd done the work, but I didn't have anyone in my corner letting everyone know I was the one who'd done it. In meeting after meeting, managers passed off my ideas and accomplishments as their own. More times than he could count he'd seen leaders shoot down points I'd raised in one meeting only to raise those exact points in the next.

In all my preparations for this position, no one warned me about this. I'd been told that if you work hard, rewards will come to you. Convinced by the rhetoric of meritocracy, I went to great lengths to rise according to nothing but my merits. Standing in Tom's office was the first time I realized that merit didn't mean much without credit. Persuaded by the slogans about refusing help and making it on my own, I never realized what my counterparts knew all along: it's easier to pride yourself on refusing handouts when you have plenty of people offering you a hand up.

Stunned by my naivete, I stood in that executive office and realized it would never be mine. I looked out that wall of windows overlooking the city. I saw the view of the skyline that stretched forever onto a world I had never seen, which served as the backdrop for the desks of so many executives who spent their careers with their backs to it, never even realizing it was ever there at all.

At Generic Corp., other than Tom, there wasn't a single person willing to speak or stand up for me. I wasn't expecting anyone to give me a free lunch. I just assumed they'd give me what I earned—credit for my own thoughts. If I could be called entitled, it would be for being presumptuous enough to assume my supervisors wouldn't steal.

To give hardworking, smart, and deserving people a chance to see for the first time all the horizons that have always been at their backs, sometimes the only thing they need is a mentor willing to share the view.

The Importance of Mentoring

In "Why Diversity Programs Fail: And What Works Better," sociology professors Frank Dobbin and Alexandra Kalev discuss how few strategies ingrain the virtues of inclusion more than mentorships. They note these relationships are "another way to engage managers and chip away at their biases. In teaching their protégés the ropes and sponsoring them for key training and assignments, mentors help give their charges the breaks they need to develop and advance. The mentors then come to believe that their protégés merit these opportunities—whether they're white men, women, or minorities. That is cognitive dissonance—'Anyone I sponsor must be deserving'—at work again."

Beyond these psychological benefits for individuals, mentoring has structural benefits for organizations. These programs diversify managerial positions as much as 24 percent. While only 10 percent of firms have mentoring programs, those that do end up experiencing profound benefits. For example, in a five-year period, Coca-Cola saw 80 percent of all protégés advance at least one level in the organization. In a six-year period, the number of Black salaried employees grew from 19.7 percent to 23 percent and the number of professionals from this group took just four years to rise from 12 percent to 15.5 percent.

With few resources and even fewer people in strategic relationships, mentoring can bring the kinds of diversity that organizations seek. These arrangements require no change to handbooks or policies. They don't require the enormous buy-in that most DEI work requires. But they have the deep impact when it comes to creating equitable structures that advance minority members.

Numerous studies have found that more than anything else mentoring is the strategy that leads to greater inclusion. Many organizations have diversity initiatives that lead to them hire more people from marginalized groups, but companies that see diversity beyond entry-level positions are those that program interactions between experts and protégés. The hard work of diverse individuals and the revised policies of leaders can create more equitable opportunities, but the individualized attention and advice that comes from mentoring makes the difference.

Despite all the claims to being data driven, evidence based, and grounded in metrics, many of the decisions regarding who gets promoted come from much simpler measurements. Performance appraisals can look at job performance in relationship to organizational objectives, but there is no denying that an uncomfortably high portion of these judgments rests on that always pervasive yet ever murky category of likability. Few can help people cross social divides to achieve the "likability" essential to professional advancement like a mentor who's already attained that status.

Steps for Inclusivity

1. DEVELOP STRUCTURES THAT MAKE INTERCULTURAL MENTORSHIPS POSSIBLE.

Avoid the problem of assuming every underrepresented team member needs a mentor. This presupposition can appear condescending and insulting. At the same time, you can't expect individuals to overcome intercultural differences and anxieties to create intercultural relationships on their own.

The best scenarios are those where mentorship opportunities are formalized. Create an official mentorship program. Let all team members know it exists. Share information about it across the board so no individuals feel singled out. Strongly encourage participation, but be careful about requiring it. Compulsory programs can create resentment by those who feel forced to join. Forcing every employee from a marginalized community to become a protégé can imply that you assume they need remedial training. Such mandates can also reduce quality as mentors or mentees grudgingly go through a program they were forced to join. If possible, publicize universally, but make it voluntary.

2. NORMALIZE MENTORSHIP AS AN ESSENTIAL PART OF PROFESSIONAL DEVELOPMENT.

Convincing a prospective protégé can take some work. You must persuade them to find the time and energy to participate in yet another activity on top of the many others competing for their time. In the case of marginalized communities, the mere thought of seeking a mentor can be intimidating. Society tells them that they don't belong, and majority members have made it on their own. Many have learned that if they want to belong, they must work twice as hard as their counterparts. To succeed in any way that will earn the respect of their peers, they feel pressured to deny all forms of assistance. This extraordinary pressure to be self-made can drive many from minority groups to avoid even the most common forms of professional advancement like networking, social events, and asking for help.

At the same time, people who come from underrepresented groups place a high priority on formal education. First-generation professionals who were also first-generation college students tend to value this kind of training. Those who grew up learning that college was the key to professional success may also feel it's the only legitimate form of success. Tap into this respect for formal education, and respect possible fears regarding informal advancement. Convince minority members to become protégés by also convincing them that it's a legitimate form of professional development.

Advertise mentoring programs as another form of professional development that is as natural, formal, and fundamentally democratic as going to college. The language around mentorship can suggest philanthropy and pity. To encourage greater participation among minority members, focus on terms about responsibility, education, and professional development. Take great strides to replace the suggestion that mentorships are something impostors need with the explanation that they are something true professionals always do.

3. REFRAME MENTORSHIPS IN TERMS OF LEGACY.

Leaders might resist DEI as a political act of charity that doesn't have a place in business. Even if they are convinced enough by the business case for inclusion, they might relegate it to HR. To get leaders personally involved, concentrate on mentorships. But remember that people have competing demands on their time and energy. Push these opportunities to the front of people's minds by showing how mentorships can give them something other opportunities cannot. Promotions and positions might provide more money, power, or prestige, but mentorships can leave a legacy. Show how taking personal responsibility for and interest in an individual can create fulfillment that other metrics cannot. Compliment prospective mentors by appealing to their knowledge, experience, and expertise. Show how much they will add value to the lives of others, the organization, and themselves.

4. PROVIDE SUPPORT.

Give participants stipends so they can attend national conferences or association retreats. Find funding to bring in guest speakers and trainers. If money's thin, cover the cost of food. If you're on a shoestring budget, give the resource of time, designating blocks of scheduling at regular intervals where participants can easily attend. For example, make it clear that lunchtime during every first Thursday of the month is when mentors and mentees connect. Protect that time from other demands.

Another way to resource these groups is to tie them to promotion. Restructure performance reviews so people are rewarded for participating in these programs. Redefine reward structures so leaders get credit for advancing others and mentees get recognized for professional development. In addition to congratulating managers for what they seem to have accomplished on their own, create criteria that reward them even more for the accomplishments they've helped others achieve. Instead of constantly celebrating the short-term gains of individuals, create point systems that applaud the long-term gains that legacy building and intergenerational training leave on the entire organization. Retool criteria for advancement, promotions, and raises so scoring systems give more weight to mentoring.

In "Won't You Be My Mentor?," Kate Mason, consultant with eMentorConnect, recommends a unique approach to creating mentor programs. She recommends asking executives to nominate management employees to be mentors. According to her, "these nominees will feel the dual pressure and reward of being chosen by their boss, and will see this opportunity as a chance to grow." Show leaders that becoming a mentor can get them promoted. Package programs in terms of shared success that benefits both protégés and mentors. Create value propositions that turn prospective advisers from reluctant participants to enthusiastic supporters. Whatever you do, don't just invite would-be mentors. Pitch mentorship in ways that show them the benefits.

Provide logistical support that makes the process as easy as possible. Don't just wait for mentorships to happen. Create a schedule for the year and send frequent reminders to increase participation and effectiveness. Compile a collection of training, resources, and readings to help people prepare. Scaffold meetings in ways that show a clear progression in purpose, scope, and challenge across the year. To maximize participation, do whatever you can to create a situation where mentors and mentees need to focus only on the relationship. Increase the likelihood that mentorships will continue by doing all you can to provide all the logistical support.

5. START WITH A COHORT MODEL.

The ideal mentoring programs might be one-on-one relationships. But this arrangement usually happens when an individual approaches another in a self-selected pairing. However, White men are more likely to seek out White men as mentors, and White men are more likely to agree to mentoring White men. In this context, inter-identity mentorships don't just happen, and organizations can wait for people from different social groups to voluntarily create mentorships.

At the same time, when creating opportunities for inter-identity mentorships, you can't rush into pairing mentors and mentees. Inter-identity, one-on-one mentorships have great potential but also great risks. An executive who's oblivious to how much heterosexual privilege has shielded him from homophobia could pressure a lesbian mentee to come out in ways that undermine her professional advancement. A manager unaware of her tendency to fall into saviorism could think she's helping an immigrant employee feel like they belong when she's actually infantilizing him in ways that drive him away.

To secure the potential of inter-identity memberships and avoid its risks, create a large pool of candidates, but don't rush to pair up people. Instead, schedule programming to bring all potential protégés and advisers together. Hold meetings where leaders present, teach, and run seminars. Create networking opportunities for mentors to learn from one another. Ensure mentees have the chance to do the same. Improve participation by having a larger number of people, creating motivation to keep up with the group. Alleviate the pressure of intense one-on-ones by having cohorts meet with one another. Use anonymous surveys to give participants the opportunity to pose questions they wouldn't dare ask over coffee with a single mentor. Feature guest speakers and expert presentations that can serve as conversation starters.

Also use this pilot period to screen participants. Pay attention to which leaders would make the best mentors. Start scrutinizing which pairings would make the most sense. Create opportunities for protégés and leaders to request certain matchups, but spend plenty of time considering these pairings so you can maximize value once you finally get to the one-on-one relationships.

6. PROVIDE TRAINING.

Don't assume people know how to mentor just because they want to, and don't presume being a mentee doesn't require any more preparation than passively accepting pearls of wisdom. Teach mentors best practices on how to listen, assess, and give appropriate advice. Teach mentees best practices on how to reflect, assess, and advocate for their own needs. Give training that focuses on these best practices, but keep them informal enough to let people fill in according to their personal experience.

Create the shell for a course, and let potential mentors and mentees populate it. Even if you don't have enough people to develop a large cohort, don't assume everyone who wants to be a mentor or mentee knows how to be one. Work together with participants to decide on an outline of topics to cover. Establish clear rules of confidentiality so people can feel comfortable sharing information without fear that it will get out to the wrong people. Leave room for participants to vent their frustrations, but also provide guidelines for conversation so meetings are productive.

Whether or not you develop a cohort model, schedule times for mentors to share strategies with one another, and give space for mentees to do the same. Dedicate some training to intercultural communication so both parties can understand how minority-majority mentorships might differ from other kinds. Ensure that older White cishet men know that what worked for them might not work for people who are younger, ethnic minorities, LGBTQ+ people, or women.

7. DEVOTE PART OF THE MENTORING TIME TO PROJECT-BASED LEARNING.

Mentorships should have room for questions about soft skills, company culture, and office politics. It's also valuable to leave room for emotional debriefs, psychological self-care, and venting. The mentorship programs that sustain over time, however, also incorporate clear opportunities for professional advancement. Create these occasions by scheduling time for projects. Foreground cooperative sessions where participants work together on focused projects during their personal time with others. Entire cohorts, small groups, or just a mentor-mentee pair could work on a proposal together. If an employee has a unique understanding of an emerging market but has no space in their regular set of duties to complete a coherent plan, these workshops could be an opportunity to draft those strategies along-side senior leaders.

Challenge mentees to incorporate the completed project as part of their normal workload. In this situation, mentorships become a place for not only psychological belonging and cultural understanding but also professional advancement. Moonlighting to create these projects with an executive sponsor helps protégés complete the project, improve its quality, and earn the blessing of higher-ups before it is even finished. Approaching mentorship meetings as a kind of thought incubator provides structure that increases participation. It also produces tangible results that can demonstrate the program's clear deliverables.

8. CAREFULLY CREATE OPPORTUNITIES FOR PAIRINGS.

Once you've determined the purpose of the program, construct a process for matching mentors and mentees. Some who volunteer to be mentors have skills that would be better used elsewhere. Some team members who think they want a particular mentor might pick the very person who could sink their career. Because these relationships have such high stakes, try to pilot the cohort mentorship model for as long as possible. During that time, note who might work best with whom. Toward the last quarter of the cohort stage, build in structures to start pairing up participants.

Devise strategies regarding what to do with volunteers who might have some growing to do before entering the one-on-one stage. What if there's a protégé who is extraordinarily willing to share personal problems and criticisms of organizational leadership? Putting them in a mentorship situation full of informal conversations might inadvertently create opportunities for them to sabotage their career. What if there's a mentor who has a heart of gold but provides overly cavalier advice? The bold strategies that worked for them might seal the fate of anyone else who tried to replicate them. Again, figure out ways to make this strategic realignment seem impersonal and procedural so participants don't feel slighted.

A possible process might include the following: Form a kind of matching committee. Protégés who have made it through the entire cohort stage write to the committee, requesting their top three picks for mentors along with a rationale for each. Mentors do the same with their top three picks for mentees. The committee reviews the proposals and considers extenuating circumstances the proposals overlooked (time constraints, competing demands, potential for personality conflict, etc.).

At this stage, committee members should devote significant discussion to the social identities of mentors and mentees. If the goal of the program is to create intercultural mentoring opportunities, make sure pairings achieve this goal. Note the well-documented tendency for mentors and mentees to gravitate toward people like them, and find ways to encourage mentorships across social identities. Also, draw from any of the psychometric assessment data the company might have to consider personality styles. Be intentional about matching both social identities and personalities.

For inter-identity pairings, hold meetings for training where people can hear from experts on topics like DEI, mentorships in general, inter-identity mentorships in particular, professional development, and personal development. Create a strategy for dealing with misalignment. Institute a process if pairings don't work out, and formalize it so changes don't seem like personal reprimands.

9. CONSIDER MENTORSHIPS BEYOND YOUR ORGANIZATION.

Intra-organizational mentorships are beneficial because they give advice that helps provide background information on a particular company, but they can also lead to restrictions. Mentees from underrepresented groups are less likely to be fully candid with leaders of their organization. According to a study led by Audrey Murrell, associate professor of business administration, psychology, and public and international affairs at the University of Pittsburgh, even when mentors invite honest responses and questions, people from marginalized communities experience hesitation. Fearing retribution, they censor themselves in ways that can keep them from experiencing the full benefits of being a protégé.

To circumvent these restrictions, Murrell's group of scholars introduced inter-organizational formal mentoring (IOFM). They define this concept as "formal mentoring activities, programs, or experiences that cut across traditional organizational boundaries and target the unique developmental needs of a specific stakeholder or identity group." In some cases, minority members can match with mentors from their social group if their organization has none. In others, they can pair with majority members from other businesses, and the fact that the latter has no authority over the former can yield more honest questions and more helpful advice. In many situations, IOFMs can be a valuable addition to mentorships that already exist within an organization, giving mentees the opportunity to hear both insider and outsider perspectives.

IOFMs also provide people in senior leadership the rare opportunity to hear the perspectives of junior employees from underrepresented communities. Because these team members have less to lose by being honest with leaders from another organization, these arrangements give IOFM mentors unique chances to hear honest feedback regarding how their leadership might affect diverse employees. Given these possibilities, Murrell et al. found that inter-organizational mentorships can provide the connections, "social capital," and "legitimacy" for underrepresented groups. Ultimately, even when people from underrepresented groups found networks outside their organizations, they had greater retention within their organizations.

IOFMs also present options for smaller organizations. If you don't have the resources to implement the steps we've detailed so far, create opportunities to meet with mentors in other organizations. Perhaps you don't have enough people to create a thriving cohort. Consider developing a network with similar companies to sponsor a network of mentors and protégés across multiple institutions in ways that benefit everyone.

10. MOVE BEYOND MENTORSHIP TO SPONSORSHIP.

Awhile into the one-on-one mentorships, train mentors on becoming sponsors. Note that mentors provide advice, but sponsors give support. The former engages with protégés during their individual meetings, but the latter elevates them during business meetings. Executive vice presidents of Coqual Pooja Jain-Link and Julia Taylor

Kennedy claim the key difference between the two comes down to risk. On the one hand, mentors give ideas, and if those suggestions don't work, the mentor suffers alone. On the other hand, sponsors put their name on the line in support of a charge, willing to stake their reputation. They call in favors to ensure the ideas, profile, and opportunities of an underrepresented person advance.

Help mentors identify whether they can become sponsors. Ensure they know how to do so. Create opportunities for them to make this transition. For example, after they've had time establishing themselves as mentors, schedule a meeting to discuss the possibility of their coauthoring projects with a protégé. Detail how sponsorships help protégés advance, help sponsors create lasting impact, and help organizations evolve in ways nothing else can.

11. BECOME A MENTOR.

Whether you're the CEO of a large company or a team member of a small organization who only has a few months on the job, take inventory of your position and the opportunities it affords. If you are a White cishet male non-disabled senior leader, sponsor someone who isn't one of these things. The research shows many in positions of power only mentor people like them. DEI allies fear making mistakes so much that they avoid intercultural mentorships as much as their DEI-resistant peers. So if you've been in your organization thirty years longer or just three months longer than a person from a marginalized group, you have some institutional knowledge others don't. Whether you're five rungs up the ladder or a few inches below the first step, you've got some advice to offer someone coming in at the ground level.

Literature suggests mentorships are among the most effective DEI strategies. Less researched is the fact that these programs are also among the most efficient and economical. They don't require divisive changes to an internal policy. They don't necessitate controversial messaging. In fact, they need little more than an individual willing to use their privilege to help someone who doesn't have it.

12. BECOME A MENTEE.

When it comes to mentorships, too many imagine a unilateral flow of knowledge. They assume mentors do all the teaching and none of the learning. But those who truly want to benefit protégés become protégés. Those who want to improve their mentorship become a mentee.

If you feel the same anxiety about an intercultural arrangement that keeps so many sponsoring their own kind, enter an arrangement where you learn about underrepresented experiences from a member of a different social group. Seek to learn under a diverse person in your organization who has a position of authority over you. Contact peers from marginalized communities who hold equal titles of authority in organizations other than your own. Hire consultants, coaches, or inter-organizational colleagues to learn about social identity in the workplace from someone who isn't beholden to you. The studies suggest the playing field would level fast if more majority members sponsored people from different groups and that the only thing holding potential allies from entering these relationships is fear. So get over the fear of being an intercultural mentor by becoming an intercultural mentee.

"Share the View"

At Generic Corp., I stood in the elevator and watched the doors close to Tom's office. My mind was swirling with anger, confusion, and sadness. I felt like a fool for believing all the rhetoric about meritocracy. I felt ashamed for believing all the people who accused DEI of reverse discrimination. I was mortified for believing majority members were as self-made as they insisted they were. I had swallowed the Gospel of Hard Work in its entirety and broke my back trying to roll boulders up the hill only to realize that the leaders in positions I wanted to occupy didn't work harder. They worked smarter. And they were smart enough to realize that all the sweat equity in the world wouldn't accomplish much without a little added mentorship.

As the elevator dinged, I felt all these emotions overtake me. While the doors started to close, I experienced a rush of realizations about myself. But even in this moment when I should've been focusing all my fury into something productive, I couldn't help but notice the sun shining through the wall of windows behind Tom's desk. Afternoon sun in the Midwest winter blares bright, but I realized then why that glorious light caught my eye. It was because it shone on the back of an executive who didn't even realize it was there.

Those metal doors shut, and the elevator began to descend onto the windowless floor that housed my cubicle. But the executives who had stolen my ideas and even the only one who had the decency to tell me they were doing so? They took for granted a picture of the horizon that I never knew existed before that meeting.

So what's the point of mentorship? What role does it play in the space of DEI? Why is it among the most powerful strategies for creating inclusion and structural change? Mentoring recognizes the horizon that's always been at your back and appreciates it for the first time. It invites others out of the cubicles and to the wall of windows. It doesn't deny that vista exists. It doesn't harp about how deserved the office is. The inclusive leader facilitates mentorships that create opportunities for people to share the view.

CHAPTER NINE

Meetings
"These Kinds of Meetings Are Everything"

I n mid-June 2020, I pressed the link to the virtual meeting with ten invitees to outline the presentation I would deliver the following week to five thousand employees at what I'll call Common Corp. The call included eight members of Common Corp.'s DEI leadership team. One led the company's LGBTQ+ employee resource group. Another was a member of its Latinx rising-stars program. A White woman was VP of a major division. But the call featured one other person I'll call Carl. And among that diverse group, Carl was the only person who was a CEO, a White male . . . and able to talk.

For most of the meeting, he discussed the importance of diversity. When I asked if we could go around and have everyone introduce themselves, he interrupted three of the eight people with non sequiturs assuring me that the organization had launched all kinds of initiatives to create equitable structures. When I finally got a word in to mention the outline that was supposed to be the focus of the meeting, he concluded the meeting by declaring, "Of course, these kinds of meetings are everything."

I appreciate Carl's enthusiasm. The fact that the CEO of such a large organization took time out of his busy schedule for a DEI meeting is impressive. At the same time, however, I worry about what these meetings suggest. They often suggest leaders are so unaccustomed to taking a back seat that they feel compelled to run meetings that aren't theirs. Some listen so infrequently that they talk incessantly, even about topics they don't understand. Others spend so little time being the only one of their social group in a meeting that they subconsciously ensure they're the only one who talks during the meeting. Finally, there are many who spend entire meetings talking about the virtues of inclusion . . . all the while excluding others from saying a single word.

Overhauling hiring, onboarding, and review policies can make a company more inclusive, but a company can only be as inclusive as its meetings. Meetings are the most common form of group interaction your organization has. They are its mass and pledge of allegiance. They are the ceremonies that most frequently and profoundly give team members the opportunity to practice the values of the team.

Want to change your organization? Change your meetings. Want employees to manage their biases? Change your meetings. Want to rid your workplace of microaggressions? Change your meetings. Want underrepresented people to have the opportunity to show their skills in ways that help them advance and diversify leadership? Change your meetings. Want to find ways to reap the benefits of inclusion? Change your meetings. Because even as a well-intentioned CEO once taught me, "meetings are everything."

The Importance of Meetings

Meetings play an important role in professional life. In 2016, professor of global leadership Rob Cross and psychologists Reb Rebele and Adam Grant found that the amount of time people spend in them "has ballooned by 50 percent or more." That same year, journalist Virginia Heffernan noted "fifteen percent of an organization's time is spent in meetings, and every day, the transcontinental conference room known as the white-collar United States plays host to 11 million meetings" and wastes "$37 billion in 'unproductive meetings.'" During the COVID-19 pandemic, these numbers climbed with people attending 13 percent more meetings. In short, meetings are important because they constitute a greater portion of our professional lives.

In addition to their frequency, meetings are important because they have an enormous impact on company culture. In "Meetings Matter: Effects of Team Meetings on Team and Organizational Success," Simone Kauffeld and Nale Lehmann-Willenbrock analyzed twenty organizations looking to pinpoint the factors that most affected company productivity. Many assume material concerns like pay, benefits, and other incentives do the most to influence productivity. Others suspect structural issues like leadership, messaging, and board oversight are the keys to a business's future. But according to Kauffeld and Lehmann-Willenbrock, indicators of company health like market share, innovation, and employment stability were tied to meeting behaviors. Tangents, rants, and criticizing can seem like insignificant and inevitable parts of work life, but the study showed these small issues led to the interpersonal problems that cause the organizational catastrophes. Their conclusion? Many of the problems and opportunities that capture the attention of leaders often stem from the meeting dynamics they often ignore.

The importance of meetings is even more pronounced when it concerns people from different social backgrounds. Associate professor of organizational behavior Victoria L. Brescoll analyzed how gender dynamics influence meetings, and found traditional exchanges privilege men. Female executives who talk during meetings receive 14 percent lower ratings for competence, while their male counterparts receive 10 percent higher ratings for the same behavior. Leaders can espouse the benefits of diversity all they want, but they'll only realize those gains if they create platforms to showcase a diversity of thought in meetings.

Plenty of people think meetings are fine if no obvious problems arise. According to this thinking, if sessions don't devolve into a melee of epithets or grounds for a discrimination lawsuit, things are good. But inclusive leaders go deeper to recognize the status quo isn't as equitable as it seems. Just because there doesn't seem to be anything wrong with your meetings doesn't mean there's anything right with them. For those waiting to change their meetings until *they* see a problem with the meeting, co-founder of Spark Decks Eva Jo Meyers and founder of Shifting Hearts & Minds Adria Husband point out, "When we default to letting our meetings run themselves, we fall into the trap of maintaining the status quo, which favors the dominant 'norm,' (usually white, male, cis-gendered, heteronormative, etc.)."

These broader assertions are supported by the specific data. Award-winning psychologist Dolly Chugh claims, "The higher-power, more extroverted, majority-demographic people are more likely to take up disproportionate airtime, receive credit, be given the benefit of the doubt and interrupt others." In a study of 360-degree feedback from one thousand female executives, Kathryn Heath and Brenda F. Wensil of Flynn Heath Holt Leadership found women are "more than twice as likely to be interrupted in group dialogue" and more likely to be discouraged from even speaking in the first place.

If promotions, advancement, and raises are based on job performance, they are also based on performativity. It's not enough to accomplish tasks behind the scenes. To prove whether someone is leadership material, they must also demonstrate leadership skills in a group setting. Meetings seem to provide a frequent glimpse of how well one can command a team. They function like auditions. They serve as interviews. Of course, the outwardly professed criteria for these decisions are characteristics like "engagement," "involvement," and "leadership potential," but the inwardly confessed yardstick for these traits can come down to meetings and who talks the most, the loudest, and the longest.

Reports, statistics, and hard data might appeal to one's rationality, but as we've explored in chapters on recruiting, hiring, and onboarding, the mind also looks for shortcuts in the form of gut reactions. Objective data is rare, numerical, and cold. Intuition looks for frequent, interpersonal, and emotional cues. In this context, a handful of group conversations can be more important than reports. Key criteria can be less convincing than a few minutes of conferencing. While interviews are powerful when it comes to someone's chances for promotion, they can pale in comparison to the persuasive evidence that can come from a single exchange between people in a meeting.

Given how important meetings are and how disadvantageous

traditional ones can be to underrepresented groups, inclusive leaders must improve their processes.

Steps for Inclusivity

1. COLLECT DATA.

Academic studies analyze trends across thousands of people, hundreds of organizations, and dozens of countries. Beyond these broad findings, do some research of your own to assess the meetings within your particular organization. Smartphone applications like Time to Talk and GenderEQ can provide empirical data regarding how much men or women talk during your meetings. They try to determine the sex of speakers and begin tracking how much time men speak as opposed to women.

With a click of a button on the website aramentalkingtoomuch .com, users can manually track how much "a dude" is speaking versus "not a dude." You can also use this dual-timer format to measure how much gay, trans, disabled, and veteran men as well as men of color get shut out of the conversation. If all else fails, create your own tally system, ticking marks beside different categories every time a desired interaction does or doesn't happen. Whatever you do, to start making meetings more inclusive, collect data.

2. BE INTENTIONAL ABOUT SCHEDULING.

If you want diversity of thinking within a meeting, plan it in ways that give people a chance to provide informed opinions. Schedule far in advance so participants can collect their thoughts. If you send an invite on short notice, people might perceive it as a power move, as though you're inviting them into a discussion for which they couldn't possibly prepare just to ensure you're the smartest person in the room.

When scheduling, also consider time complications like the age, ability, socioeconomic, childcare, and health status of invitees. If you value the opinions of working parents, avoid scheduling meetings before school starts or after it lets out. If you really want insights from people across the socioeconomic spectrum, don't slate meetings for when people might be working their second job. If you crave the wisdom of team members from across the world, diplomatically set meetings according to different time zones. Rarely is there a perfect time that works for everyone, but be thoughtful and intentional about your scheduling, keeping in mind that the social groups that can attend the meeting might depend on when you schedule it.

3. SCRUTINIZE WHERE YOU HOLD MEETINGS.

Even before you start a meeting, be mindful about how the setting can affect your attempts to be inclusive. Some ideas to consider:

1. Is the meeting room in an accessible location in the building?
2. Even if your office has universal accessibility, how will the meeting room affect attendance?
3. Even if elevators and ramps comply with laws that make locations physically accessible, consider psychological comfort. If you're holding meetings on your turf on the top floor, will entry-level workers feel too intimidated to attend? If you're

trying to meet people where they are by meeting in their area, will they feel invaded?

4. Beyond thinking about the accessibility of the room, consider accessibility within the room. Is there enough seating for everyone? Are their clear spaces at the table for people who use wheelchairs? Are chairs accessible for all body types?

5. Remember virtual accessibility. If you're holding meetings online, is the technology accessible to all? Does everyone have a home situation where they can have a sustained conversation? Do all attendees have access to reliable internet connections? Does everyone have internet access at all?

6. Be careful about how your explicitly stated or heavily implied practice regarding video affects attendance. Conflating active video with participation can be classist. It privileges people who can afford to have house settings (climate, soundscapes, furniture, physical backgrounds) that conform to conventional standards of professionalism to display their video in the first place. For these reasons, be flexible about video requirements.

4. BE STRATEGIC ABOUT YOUR INVITATION LIST.

Before sending out that invitation, take stock of who's on it. Be aware that different combinations create different dynamics. Inviting John can cause Tim to shut down, whereas inviting Lisa can be the thing that makes him contribute more.

Beyond personality interactions, be aware of how different positions influence the discussion. A guest list that is predominantly white collar might cause the blue-collar team members to clam up.

Attendance by a single member from the C-suite could drive everyone to jockey for position so desperately that everyone talks and no one listens.

In addition to considering personalities and positions, also think about social identity. When was the last time you were in a situation where you were the only person from your group? What did it feel like? How did it affect your contribution to conversation? Be aware of your answers to these questions when deciding your invitees. Of course, this isn't to say that you can only invite women to meetings where they are the majority. In many organizations, this line of logic would mean women wouldn't get invited to any meetings at all. By definition, underrepresented people will be outnumbered in most situations, but balance this demographic underrepresentation as much as possible with personalities that can be inclusive. Marginalized people are less likely to speak up in meetings and more likely to be spoken over. Encourage their participation by inviting fewer people that they would have to speak in front of and fewer personality types that would try to speak over them.

When defining key members, don't forget the essential but overlooked. It seems obvious, but if you're discussing issues that affect a group, you should have them be part of the discussion. If you're rewriting the policy on parental leave, invite mothers and fathers. If you don't have anyone who publicly self-identifies as trans but you want to revise your company's forms for inclusive gender identity options, hire an outside expert who can inform strategies based on best practices. Every group you're making decisions *for* should be a group you're making decisions *with*. Make sure your invitation list reflects that reality.

5. CIRCULATE THE AGENDA AHEAD OF TIME.

Inclusive meetings exchange diverse ideas. For that interaction to be as genuine as possible, everyone must have information. If you call a meeting but don't let anyone know what it's about, you've set up an ambush. You'll unload everything you've thought about regarding the topic for weeks, months, or years on end, and then save the final 5 percent of the meeting for people to contribute. They'll be reeling too much from the new information you just unloaded to provide any knowledgeable ideas. Then you'll be angry that no one contributes.

If you really want their ideas, set them up for success by giving them all the data you needed to develop your own. Provide all the reports, figures, and other supporting materials you used to become as informed as you are. Software company Atlassian has an interesting set of strategies for running more inclusive meetings. For example, it encourages team members to "list agenda items as questions, not generic topics, and encourage participants to come prepared. This gives introverts a chance to process information outside of the pressure of a loud social setting. Enlist allies (e.g., men, extroverts, etc.) to lead by example and hold them accountable for making space for their female, remote, and introverted counterparts to contribute."

Circulated agendas also give people the opportunity to plan ideas, prepare self-advocacy techniques, and practice the "engagement" and "involvement" your organization uses to assess "leadership potential." This process can allow group coordination where ignored constituents strategize ways to amplify their voices. They might brainstorm ideas before meetings and come to shared agreements so they're all on the same page. They might coordinate comments so that a more introverted person doesn't get drowned out by a more extroverted one. If there's a person who habitually interrupts others, this group can practice making sure to redirect attention back to people that are interrupted.

Disseminating agendas can also create room for the brilliant ideas that can happen asynchronously. Some of the most productive ideas can be those that contradict the most powerful people in the room. Neurodiverse people might have their best ideas in private. Letting them email their ideas ahead of time allows that thinking to come to the forefront. If someone is from an underrepresented group, they are statistically more likely to have their ideas dismissed. Creating an anonymous portal or letting people email their ideas to the meeting reporter to read while keeping names anonymous can ensure people hear ideas they otherwise never would.

Oftentimes, people balk at the idea of fixing their ideas to an agenda. Rather than structure their thoughts, they would rather wing it. Instead of admitting that they don't want to commit themselves to an outline, they usually claim they don't have time to formulate, much less circulate, agendas. If you find yourself making this excuse, collect some data. Run a series of meetings without an agenda and see how long they take. Then do the same with an agenda. In most situations, taking twenty minutes to pen an outline and having the foresight to send it out a few days ahead of the meeting can actually trim down meeting times significantly. Besides creating a greater sense of inclusion and creating more opportunities for people from underrepresented groups to participate fully, circulating agendas benefits everyone by making meetings more organized and usually quicker.

6. SHARE SPACE.

Anita Williams Woolley is an associate professor of organizational behavior and theory who sought to determine the characteristics of effective teams. Her team of researchers developed two studies with 699 people working in groups to try to discover if there was "a collective intelligence factor" that made one group's performance better than another's. They found that group intelligence had less to do with the "average or maximum intelligence of group members" than how well they equally took turns talking in conversation. According to these findings, if you want to make meetings more productive, concentrate on making discussion more egalitarian.

One way to do this is to start meetings with a round-robin. In this practice, give everyone the chance to talk once before anyone talks twice. Don't require that everyone speak. Some might have nothing to say. People with different ability statuses might be unable to speak on the spot. But start meetings with the practice of sharing space. The purpose of a meeting is to generate creative thinking, not shouting matches. If someone's got a great follow-up idea, they can wait their turn. If the idea's really that great, they'll remember it. And if an idea is truly profound, it will be just as profound when it's my turn to speak. The round-robin is both clear and playful enough to accomplish this task. It rewrites the rules of society with new rules of the meeting in ways that give underrepresented people the opportunity to contribute in a nonconfrontational, impersonal, and systematic way.

7. PRACTICE CONSTRUCTIVE DISSENT.

I'm always amazed by leaders who are surprised that people won't disagree with them. They hold power over people's pay, advancement, and livelihood yet are confused as to why people won't tell them the truth. In meetings like the one I had with Carl, the most powerful can be the least informed. Time and again, I've witnessed scenarios where everyone knew the reality of the situation but couldn't bring themselves to tell decision makers. What's worse is that the Carls of the world spend untold fortunes to crunch data for solutions people around them already could share if only their leaders could stop talking. But you can't just trust people to share their ideas. What about organizational structure incentivizes disagreeing with the powerful? Furthermore, what about the history of the business world would motivate people from underrepresented groups to speak up? Dissent, constructive dissent, the kind of dissent that could grow your business, the kind of dissent that could save you from yourself is already sitting around your conference table. You must create structures that encourage, protect, and foster it.

Go beyond passively excusing dissent to actively encouraging it. At the same time, you have to ensure that inviting dissent doesn't create a structure where people in positions of privilege just use that climate to continue blocking out marginalized voices. So how do you invite minority members to contradict majority members without simultaneously causing counteractive statements to balloon in ways that further alienate the former? One way is to systematize it. Like the round-robin has a name, rules, and practice that makes it seem like a harmless game, restructure meetings in an impersonal, quick, and clear way by assigning a devil's advocate. This activity makes dissent seem less personal than procedural. If you wait for contradictions to happen, they won't. In the off chance that they do, if you don't have a system in place that requires them, those disagreements will seem like surprising power plays one individual unleashes on another. To systematize this process, assign a person to play devil's advocate throughout the entire meeting, giving the express duty to offer counterpoints to everyone.

Even better than giving this responsibility to one person is requiring it of all people, but you can't let it be a free-for-all of constant contradiction. You can designate a portion of the meeting for "upside-down time." After spending one section of the meeting coming up with ideas, designate another for nothing but inversion. This process normalizes diversity of thought and helps every team member develop these critical thinking skills.

In addition to assigning this role to one person throughout an entire meeting or to all people during one portion of the meeting, you could structure meetings in ways that require people to debate themselves. Walt Whitman's famous poem "Song of Myself" contains a stunning passage that reads, "Do I contradict myself? / Very well then I contradict myself, / (I am large, I contain multitudes.)" Make a game of things by evoking this passage from "Song of Myself" by calling for people to "sing it," a shorthand invitation that pressures people to contradict themselves. This game invites players to reframe self-contradiction as proof of large and multitudinous thinking. This "sing it" game also encourages people to think more creatively by rewarding them for critiquing their own ideas.

Most important, whether you use upside-down time or the sing-it game, redefine what it means to play devil's advocate. In modern practice, the term has devolved into little more an excuse for people in positions of power to shoot down the ideas of marginalized people without looking cruel for doing so. As when people say, "No offense," before saying something totally offensive, many use the phrase "just playing devil's advocate" for an excuse to belittle, demean, and dismiss others. Even when these power asymmetries don't exist, playing devil's advocate has often come to mean little more than negating everything while positing nothing. But a true devil's advocate should do more than respond to argument A with argument "not A," which does little more than leave a void. More than tearing down a popular opinion, being a devil's advocate means praising an unpopular one. After all, the term "devil's advocate" means to advocate *for* the devil, not necessarily *against* anything.

To invite dissent while retaining civility, structure playing devil's advocate, upside-down time, and the sing-it game in ways in which people don't disparage a viewpoint as much as espouse another. If a person argues for oranges, the sing-it game would require they *also* argue for apples. If the group spends forty minutes brainstorming how to paint the room gray, response time would have them *also* spend a few minutes brainstorming how to paint it blue. The point is not to invite opposition as much as it is to foster multiplicity, to not simply shoot down ideas but propose additional ideas. If Latasha explains the virtues of oranges, it's not enough for Tom to simply point out the problems with them. Both Latasha and Tom must also point out the benefits of apples.

To run inclusive meetings that encourage a diverse range of ideas in ways that are productive rather than counteractive, structure games that invite dissent without seeming personal but also remain creative enough to be constructive.

8. RETURN TO THE INTERRUPTED.

Among all the legally permissible activities in the workplace, one of the most damaging to underrepresented people is interruptions during meetings. When majority members steamroll their minority counterparts, it makes the latter seem passive. Conversely, when the tables are turned and marginalized groups do the same thing, they are seen as overly aggressive. These discussion patterns affect decisions regarding who seems assertive enough to deserve promotions, raises, and advancement.

Because of how devastating disruptions can be, they become one of the many things an inclusive meeting should exclude. Meetings privilege people who talk the most, loudest, and longest, but fantastic ideas can also come from those who don't even get a chance to speak. If you want meetings where the smartest, wisest, and most innovative thinking comes to the fore, create structures so quieter people also have room to speak despite interruption.

To start this process, draft a strategy, write a script, and practice ways to return to the interrupted. That way, when interruptions happen in the moment, your reaction will be automatic and won't require you to muster great amounts of bravery. Also, you'll be able to respond to interruptions so seamlessly that they will swiftly put others on notice. At the same time, shutting down these infractions with rehearsed precision will avoid needlessly mortifying interrupters you still need for an inclusive conversation.

Here are some favorites:

- I would love to include the ideas from everyone in the group. [INSERT NAME], what are your thoughts?

- Thanks so much for that thought. I think that [INSERT NAME] was also trying to add an idea. What were you about to say, [INSERT NAME]?
- Before we move on, let's pause to see if anyone has any other ideas. Let's go around the room, starting with [INSERT NAME].
- To be sure that we do get out all of the ideas, let's let everyone talk without interruption.

Whether you stop the interruption or let it run its course, the point isn't to reprimand the interrupter as much as it is to return to the interrupted.

If you're a person who constantly gets interrupted and no one comes to your aid, there are a few tips for taking the floor. In "How to Manage Interruptions in Meetings," executive coach and author Harrison Monarth reminds people to acknowledge differential power dynamics. People tend to think leaders who interrupt are assertive and others who do the same are rude. Given this fact, he urges people to recognize the context when trying to take the floor back from someone who's interrupted them. In all situations, he lays down some basic principles. Among them are to let interrupters know you hear them and will return to them after you finish your point.

In addition to these strategies for returning to the interrupted, one of the best strategies is being proactive. If you know someone is an excitable extrovert with hyperactive energy and overwhelming enthusiasm that compels them to interrupt, don't squelch them. Redirect them. Jim might not have a malicious bone in his body. While many interrupt people to discount their ideas, he might interrupt them because he so fervently agrees with them. Despite his best intentions, if he speaks over Lourdes, he still has the impact of amplifying his voice and minimizing hers. In these cases, find something else to do with their energy. Have them lead, facilitate, or transcribe the meeting. Assign another, equally important, and parallel task at the same time as the meeting but that happens someplace other than the meeting. Give them ways to use their dynamism for the good of the team but in a context that saves them from themselves being detrimental to the team.

9. KEEP CREDIT WHERE IT'S DUE.

In "Women, Find Your Voice," Kathryn Heath, Jill Flynn, and Mary Davis Holt find one of the most common ways men sabotage the careers of women is by repackaging ideas. They found most women experience moments where they plan for days, prepare supporting materials, and articulate a thorough position only to have a man who hadn't prepared for the meeting simply rephrase their ideas and make them sound like his own.

To stave off credit thieves, craft, draft, and practice your response. It doesn't have to be anything groundbreaking. Depending on the circumstances, it might not be in the best interest of the group to unleash a withering lecture. In certain contexts, a response might simply be to repackage the attempt at repackaging. If Lakisha articulates a brilliant plan for Q4 and Greg tries to pass it off as his own, you can simply acknowledge Greg's contribution while turning attention back to Lakisha's: "Thank you, Greg, for that great reflection of Lakisha's idea." Whatever these tactics look like, whether you're the person leading the meeting or simply an ally sick of watching this kind of theft, find creative ways to centralize the marginalized by ensuring credit remains where it is due.

10. ELEVATE IDEAS.

In addition to combating exclusionary behavior, you must create in-clusionary ones. Beyond preventing idea theft, also find ways to ele-vate thinking. If you're a leader, be intentional about elevating ideas with phrases like "that's a good idea" or "let's build on that." While the criticism of peers is harmful, the compliments of superiors can be helpful. If you're not a leader, coordinate elevation strategies. For example, if you're a woman heading into a meeting where women always get talked over, orchestrate a plan with other women to ele-vate one another's ideas so they get the recognition they deserve. Identify allies in positions of authority and share your ideas ahead of time and ask for advice or support so they'll be more likely to elevate them when it comes time for the actual meeting.

11. FOLLOW UP.

The full import of meetings doesn't fit neatly inside a specified time or conference room. It spills into the hallways, emails, and watercooler talk. These post-meeting elements are as important to interpreting the significance of a meeting as the actual scene itself.

The biases that infiltrate the meeting only worsen once the meet-ing ends. The same misperceptions that lead many participants to think Greg is brilliant when all he did was repackage Lakisha's idea will, over time, lead them to forget Lakisha ever spoke up in the meeting at all. To manage biased reflection of who said what and what the invitees decided, circulate a written document. Depending on the context, level of confidentiality, and legal restrictions, go beyond minutes to provide thorough notes. Assign a detail-oriented person who values accuracy to provide a written record of key information.

Circulate notes so there are archives about conclusions, contributions, and next steps. Invite people to review and correct them. Doing so will help people remember more factually what happened in the past. They will also remember more clearly what's required for next steps in the future. The vague category of "leadership potential" becomes a major criterion by which promotions are decided. Meetings become a key element of that measure. A factual record of what a person has actually contributed in meetings over the last few years will help ground those decisions in facts.

12. SHARE LEADERSHIP.

Another way to elevate people is to share leadership. Meyers and Husband recommend rotating who is in charge: "Create a schedule so that everyone who attends your meetings has a chance to be the one to both finalize the agenda and facilitate the discussions." Let them know far in advance when their turn is coming. Coach them and help them prepare. Make this one of the lessons covered during mentorship programs. If meetings become a primary vehicle by which people assess the "leadership potential" of participants, become more intentional about creating opportunities for them to actually lead. Too often "engagement" and "involvement" mean little more than talking the most, the longest, and over others. Get a more accurate demonstration of how people can run a team by giving them regularly scheduled, informal, and cost-efficient auditions where they run a meeting.

"These Kinds of Meetings Are Everything"

As I logged out of the meeting where Carl dominated the conversation, I wondered how many great ideas Common Corp. has missed. How many innovations has Carl passed up because he couldn't listen? How will his company fare in a future against competitors that have learned to make their meetings inclusive enough to be innovative?

The research shows organizations improve when they have meeting structures, practices, and cultures that allow different people to share in the conversation. In the case of businesses that talk about the radical changes they want to make on behalf of inclusion, sometimes the most radical thing they can do is be quiet. In the end, if only one thing is clear from so many exchanges I've had with so many Carls, it is that "these kinds of meetings are everything."

CHAPTER TEN

Performance Reviews
"Answers from the Void"

I had been coaching Jason for months. He was the only Black employee at his organization and oversaw eighty people. He'd been working at the same place for five years but felt stalled. During one of our sessions, he grew extraordinarily frustrated, explaining that it was time for his annual evaluation. He insisted he welcomed the opportunity to take inventory, measuring successes and exploring places for growth. At the same time, after years of going through this process, he questioned its value.

And he wasn't the only one who had these doubts. According to him, no one understood these annual appraisals or how they related to advancement. The employee handbook required everyone to complete one. It stated that they were tied to promotion, but people didn't understand how. Jason claimed the process just terrified everyone into working so hard they exhausted themselves.

Having completed these kinds of reviews many times, Jason had even deeper questions. He would collect all his evidence and prepare all his talking points. Reviewers would take notes and point out things he hadn't considered, but then the report would get tossed into "the void." That's what people called it, especially those from underrepresented groups who would do all the work required for the performance reviews essential to promotion, only to somehow find themselves passed over again. According to Jason, the only ones who didn't call the review process "the void" were the same group of people who he claimed did mediocre work, showed little initiative, and had even less leadership potential but kept stumbling their way up the organizational ladder.

Jason isn't alone in this frustration. Many people from underrepresented groups suspect the performance review process is stacked against them. Those from marginalized communities can already feel impostor syndrome. They can find it demoralizing to go through a process that exposes those insecurities. Worst of all are the situations where the criteria are unclear and seem discriminatory.

Essential to retention is engagement. Fundamental to engagement is advancement. Because many organizations tie things like raises, bonuses, promotion, and even termination to the performance review process, it becomes a key element of retaining team members. At the same time, because these appraisals rely on human decision-making, they run the risk of harboring the kinds of biases that disadvantage minority communities. Therefore, we must take steps to make them more inclusive.

Oftentimes, even the leaders who achieve some diversity find it concentrated at the entry level, and even they end up wondering why there isn't greater representation in leadership. Many answers lie with performance reviews, which create a bottleneck that prevents organizations from being as inclusive as they could be. But there are strategies for clearing this logjam and tips for improving the performance review process in ways that help team members hear some answers from the void.

The Importance of Performance Reviews

In many organizations, performance reviews hold enormous power. Supervisors evaluate team members and determine future courses of action. But these appraisals have a fundamental flaw: they assume people can accurately review the performance of others. A single exercise can alter a person's livelihood and life. Giving this much power to these decisions places an enormous amount of faith in human perception, a faith that is unwarranted.

In studies that have looked at thousands of managers across three decades, more than 60 percent of ratings reflected the subjective opinions of reviewers more than the objective performance of reviewees. According to business consultant Marcus Buckingham, this "idiosyncratic rater effect" shows that leaders rate in ways that are largely projections of themselves: "My rating of you on a quality such as 'potential' is driven not by who *you* are, but instead by *my* own idiosyncrasies—how I define 'potential,' how much of it I think *I* have, how tough a rater I usually am."

These flaws worsen when we consider social identity. For example, the inaccuracies that exist between different personalities widen when evaluation occurs across racial categories. In one study, inclusion and leadership expert Arin N. Reeves circulated two sets of memos that contained the same number of errors, but one set identified the writer as "Caucasian" and the other as "African American." The former author received praise for being a "generally good writer" with "good analytical skills," while the latter got criticism that said he "needs lots of work" and was "average at best." Reviewers found an average of 2.9/7.0 spelling and grammar errors in the "Caucasian" memo as opposed to 5.8/7.0 in the "African American" one, 4.1/6.0 technical errors in the "Caucasian" sample versus 4.9/6.0 in the "African American" one, and 3.2/5.0 errors in facts for the "Caucasian" document compared to 3.9/5.0 in its "African American" counterpart. Regardless of the reviewer's race or ethnicity, even when the memo was the same, supposedly objective reviewers gave the "Caucasian" writer significantly higher praise.

Joan C. Williams, Denise Lewin Loyd, Mikayla Boginsky, and Frances Armas-Edwards also find reviewer bias in the evaluations of people from other underrepresented groups. They find that reviewers are likely to note mistakes with 43 percent of people of color and 31 percent of White women compared to 26 percent of White men. Evaluators give opposing assessments for similar actions. For example, when minority members act assertively, reviewers criticize them for being "difficult." When White men do the same, reviewers praise them for being "authoritative." They credited 50 percent of Black women for doing "office housework" compared to 16 percent of White women and 3 percent of White men. Stereotypes suggest which behaviors are common to which groups as well as which characteristics should be held by different demographics. These different responses along the lines of race and gender show the extent to which those social biases appear in professional evaluations.

Organizations that tie large rewards and punishments to these evaluations face problems when team members suspect this process is unfair. According to Melissa Phillippi, CEO of Performance Culture Inc., "If employees sense rater bias exists and do not feel rewarded fairly, their productivity may drop to 77%." Sensing these varying levels of scrutiny, majority members are more likely to underperform, supposing reviewers will take it easier on them. Suspecting the cards are stacked against them, minority members are also at risk of giving up, fearing reviewers will rake them over the coals no matter what they do.

At the same time, performance reviews can be valuable. Ratings might privilege majority members, but when organizations remove performance reviews altogether, overall worker performance drops by 10 percent and decreases engagement by 6 percent. Jackie Wiles, brand content manager at Gartner, a technology research and consulting company, finds that deleting quantitative data from the review process erodes the quality and frequency of performance conversations. The situation worsens when it comes to people from underrepresented groups. The performance review process might be biased against them, but at least it gives them warnings. When organizations remove even these flawed evaluations, BIPOC, women, and disabled people can face even greater threat of being passed over for promotions or fired without notice.

So, the challenge becomes modifying performance reviews in ways that increase engagement, improve retention, and remain fair. How, exactly, can you do this?

Steps for Inclusivity

1. INTERROGATE YOUR CURRENT REVIEW PROCESS.

Chronicle your performance review process. Examine and detail it by considering each aspect below:

1. Note who does the reviews and who gets reviewed.
2. Figure out how frequently those reviews occur and why.
3. Explain what criteria they use and who decided on them.
4. Pinpoint what reviewees are supposed to do to prepare for their review.
5. Identify what reviewers are supposed to do.
6. Specify how long the review process takes, what people do with it, and how it goes up the ladder.
7. Find out how one review relates to the next and what kind of feedback leaders give.
8. Track how this information affects promotions, raises, and other consequences.
9. Discover how this process is articulated, and differentiate between policy and practice, exposing the moments where people cut corners.

After reviewing the process, go further and gauge perception. Survey team members to see what they know about the process and how they feel about it. Do they think it's fair, biased, or something else? Clear, opaque, or a little of both? How would they improve the review process? How does it affect their productivity? Does it inspire improvement or just cause anxiety?

In addition to looking at processes and perceptions, examine criteria. These are the cornerstones of the performance review process. To inspire measurable growth, they should be specific, measurable, attainable, relevant, and time based. They should be as numerous and detailed as possible. Most important, they should be continuously improving.

No criteria are as clear as they could be. None are as uniform as we assume. Why? They are rooted in concepts, and concepts are frustratingly and inextricably subjective. Reviewers might rate a reviewee's "potential" on a scale of one to five, but if you ask them to define "potential," they'll have difficulty. Ask them to give three examples of it, and they'll have an even harder time. Gather a room of one hundred people with even the clearest definitions, and they will evaluate the potential of one team member in one thousand different ways.

For these reasons, interrogate criteria. Bring together diverse groups of stakeholders from multiple levels of your organization. Include executives, managers, board members, and reviewees. More than any other examinations, reviews are where people measure specific performance in relationship to broad goals. They are the most detailed investigation into how the organization and the individual interact. For that reason, it is important to have people from multiple levels of the organization providing input.

When interrogating how well performance reviews measure the alignment between individual performance and organizational goals, ask a lot of questions. Which criteria do we use? Why? Which others could we use? For which purposes? What does each criterion mean? Do reviewers share these definitions? Do reviewees?

Run these criteria through the Green Rabbits Graph you made in chapter 2. Home in on the definitions used in these performance reviews. Consider who constructed them. Recognize that the standards of professionalism people assume are universal often privilege some groups and disadvantage others. Explore which social groups benefit from your current criteria just by virtue of their cultural background. Examine which do not. Decide which criteria conflate personal values with professional ones.

Most important, fight the urge to say, "That's good enough." Even if your performance review processes, perceptions, and criteria are stellar, regularly set aside time to interrogate them in ways that seek to improve.

2. CLARIFY SCORING.

Many organizations use open forms. In these documents, supervisors have free rein to write what they want about a team member's performance. Some forms have a little more specificity, using a handful of prompts that are still open ended.

In response to such structures, Williams recommends taking open-form reviews and breaking them up into categories. Ensure those categories connect to broader organizational goals, mission, vision, and values. Provide rationale that clarifies those links. Under each category, provide narrow subcategories that break down those groups even more.

If the form uses numerical rankings, provide explanations for each number. Give the standard 1 equals poor and 5 equals excellent, but go further. Specify rubrics to provide examples of what a 1/poor looks like as opposed to a 5/excellent. Suppose you have a category for "initiative." Don't just give a 3, letting a reviewee know they showed average ingenuity. Instead, use a chart that stipulates people get a 3 if they have started one team program and one organization-wide program. Also explain they can get a 5 in the following year if they start three team programs and three organizational ones. Clarify both why a reviewee received the score they did and the benchmarks they could achieve to earn a higher one.

Note: We will cover how performance reviews should have a mix of numbers and narrative. While numbers have their shortcomings, they can be valuable when you average them across multiple reviews. To mitigate the bias of any individual reviewer, organizations can average scores across multiple reviewers.

3. REQUIRE EVIDENCE.

Performance review documents can determine the professional future of a reviewee. Because of their power, the burden of proof falls on the reviewers. Therefore, evaluation forms should be structured in a way that requires a preponderance of evidence. Revise them so they contain not only numerical descriptions as well as rubric explanations but also blank spaces that require specific evidence. If a manager wants to give a team member a 1 for cooperation, they should cite specific actions that prove the person's uncooperativeness. In the case of negative evaluations, the leader should also provide supporting materials from entities beyond themselves proving those actions occurred and were harmful enough to earn the reviewee such a low score.

4. STRUCTURE CRITICISM.

People from majority groups are more likely to have experiences of being socially validated. Conversely, people from underrepresented groups are more likely to be stigmatized. For example, White professionals who work in offices surrounded by people who look like them are less likely to feel impostor syndrome than their Black counterparts. One study from the *Journal of Personality and Social Psychology* found that, because of social validation or social stigmatization, members of these groups experienced criticism differently. Having years of feeling like they belong in professional settings, when White people encounter criticism, they feel their sense of belonging vary by an average of 4 percent. Conversely, spending most of their time being "the only one," Black people who encounter similar criticism see their sense of belonging shift by an average of 60 percent. Working in an office full of people who look like them makes the one group feel like they belong regardless of criticism, but doing the same in an office full of people who look different seems to prove one's suspicions that they are an outsider.

Reviewers are more likely to criticize underrepresented people, and underrepresented reviewees are more likely to experience criticism more harshly. For these reasons, leaders can balance the amount of negative and positive comments all team members receive. Instead of addressing "strengths" and "weaknesses" that have to do with a person's character, concentrate on "accomplishments" and "goals" that focus on their actions. Consider providing the same number of items for both categories no matter the reviewee. Low-performing team members won't suddenly perform better if you list all their flaws. Most likely, they'll cave in and perform even worse. Conversely, high-performing team members won't necessarily appreciate being told their review will take only thirty seconds because they've done nothing wrong.

Maximize productivity and improvement by structuring both criticism and praise. Set the expectation that everyone will get a summary that lists, say, five accomplishments and five goals. Create common expectations that train reviewers and reviewees to practice a growth mindset. No matter how many faults someone has, they will receive accomplishments to build upon. No matter how many accomplishments someone has, they will receive the same number of suggested goals. The traditional review process rewards some and punishes others, but this revised structure aims to help everyone evolve.

5. HOLD NORMING SESSIONS.

After interrogating the process and revising the structure of review forms, hold norming sessions. A few weeks before performance reviews, assemble reviewers. Remind them of the standards. Explain what each means and how they look. Go through the forms and parse out the criteria. Invite DEI trainers to review the threats of bias. Cover statistics that remind people human psychology predisposes reviewers to overpraise people from centralized groups and overcriticize people from marginalized ones. Cover things like affinity, confirmation, halo/horns, framing, and status quo bias.

Most important, create opportunity for them to practice. Assemble fictional profiles. Have reviewers use the scales, rubrics, and forms to evaluate them. Average scores into a composite evaluation so people can see how their ratings compare. If profile number one earns an average of 3.7 and Jessie gave it a 4.2, he can see the need to be a little more critical. If profile number two earns an average of 4.7 and Jessie gave it a 3.2, he can recognize the need to look for more positives. Create conversation so managers can practice explaining their evaluations and questioning others. Get them used to providing evidence and interrogating their decisions. Help them overcome biased or superficial appraisals by having someone look over their shoulder.

Beyond holding these norming sessions for reviewers, conduct them for reviewees. Norming sessions for reviewers should happen toward the end of the cycle right before they are ready to review people. Conversely, norming sessions for reviewees should happen at the beginning of the cycle so they have as much time as possible to plan their performance for the next review. In these trainings, show how evaluators scored fictional profiles. Detail the reasoning managers provided for various conclusions. The point of the review process should be to help team members grow, so give them the information they need to improve.

6. LOWER THE STAKES.

Have performance reviews more informally. Professors and experts on human resources and human capital management Peter Cappelli and Anna Tavis note that many companies are moving away from high-stakes annual review sessions to low-stakes and frequent ones. One third of US companies, including Microsoft, Deloitte, Gap, and General Electric, have replaced yearly reviews with weekly check-ins. In these situations, supervisors give instant feedback that helps team members refine their individual goals and deepen the connections between those personal objectives and organizational ones. Some even go as far as distributing small weekly bonuses to employees who achieve their goals.

Lowering the stakes of these reviews can minimize the anxiety of reviewees. Instead of crumbling under the pressure of annual appraisals, they can thrive under the direction of regular feedback. Having more frequent exchanges gives people more time to improve instead of spending a year sinking deeper into mistakes. This schedule also helps the organization avoid long stretches of underperformance because it gives managers the chance to guide people more frequently.

Lowering the stakes and increasing the frequency can mitigate the damaging biases that can appear in any single appraisal. Patterns can emerge, and problems can appear. Reviewees can have the chance to remedy errors, and reviewers can have room to justify their supposedly objective perspectives more often.

7. SCAFFOLD REVIEWS.

Imagine Nicole has seven months of low-stakes meetings where John applauds her for doing great work. Then, when it comes time for the formal review, John suddenly surprises her with a negative evaluation. Likewise, it would be unfair for Nicole to have a cycle of low-stakes reviews where John gave her nothing but praise only to end the cycle by heading into a high-stakes review where John's supervisor, Tim, suggests she should be terminated.

Find ways to keep the frequent check-ins informal enough to encourage honesty but formal enough to create consistency. Structure them in ways that foreground improvement. Require growth from one check-in to the next. Move away from thinking about reviews as an evaluation of the past, and start thinking about them as plans for the future. Instead of critiquing what people have done, concentrate on what they should do. Documenting informal check-ins like this will help reviewees progress over time and prepare for the responses they'll receive during formal performance reviews. It will also protect against the biases of any individual reviewer.

Consider the following structure:

- Every few weeks, direct managers meet for a few minutes with each individual on their team. During that time, they discuss previous goals, progress, and new objectives. Then they write up brief reports.
- Every quarter, a different set of managers reviews those reports and meets for slightly longer with people on teams other than their own to do the same.
- Finally, their superiors have the formal annual review where leaders and reviewees discuss all the documents, goals, accomplishments, and improvements for the entire year.

Whatever structure works best for your organization, strive to make it so every team member enters annual reviews without any surprises. Why? The purpose of the appraisal process isn't to make things so secretive that employees might be terrified into looking productive. The goal should be to make it so transparent that team members have enough guidance to guarantee they actually are productive.

8. EMPHASIZE SELF-REFLECTION.

Most organizations have a process where a manager evaluates an employee's work performance. Traditionally, this has been a top-down arrangement with supervisors compiling data and telling workers how they're doing, but for years, leaders have been taking steps to get the assessed more involved in the process. In the form of self-reviews, employees can correct inaccurate information, provide responses, and demonstrate more introspection.

Making self-reflection part of the performance review process has many values. It helps minimize the stress managers can feel when the burden of evaluating the worth of a human's work rests squarely on their shoulders. In addition to helping share the load, self-reflection can improve accuracy. Even the most thorough manager will underemphasize some contributions and forget others. Self-reflection can help employees discuss tasks their supervisors never knew about or provide explanations they couldn't know.

But perhaps one of the greatest benefits of incorporating self-reflection in this process is that it increases employee engagement. The Corporate Leadership Council's global study of fifty thousand employees found that workers are 87 percent less likely to leave their company when there is high employee engagement.

Few things achieve this engagement more than self-reflection. According to Michael Henckel, associate editor at J. J. Keller & Associates, "encouraging employees to give feedback on their own performance grants them partial ownership over the outcome of the final performance appraisal." They cease being passive entities subject to the whims of an assessor and become active participants in how their work is evaluated.

Asking employees what they've done well gets them in the practice of recognizing their strengths. Requiring them to write passages on how they would improve trains them to start using a growth mindset. Asking them how those accomplishments and those improvements align with the organization's objectives and values helps individuals contribute to the whole more intentionally. Written self-reflections give reviewees more of a say in the process, which improves enthusiasm. Having these documents also gives leaders a greater understanding of how the endeavors of each team member connect.

9. MAKE GOALS COLLABORATIVE.

Professors Mike Schraeder, J. Bret Becton, and Ron Portis note that people who articulate goals are more likely to achieve them. This is even truer when it comes to submitting those aspirations in written form to a supervisor. When team members have freedom to make their own goals, they are more likely to select ones they care about and can attain. The fact that they have the autonomy to pick things they value can inspire deeper commitment to them.

While self-reflection creates space for reviewees to select their own goals, the process should also be collaborative. According to Schraeder, Becton, and Portis, it's important to give employees the freedom to select some objectives, but if they have no guidance, they might choose goals that could damage their careers. At the same time, having every team member charting a course that's completely individual can lead to disarray.

To help people identify the goals that will help both them and the organization, managers should think about performance reviews more as a conversation than as an evaluation.

The central purpose should be solutions based, forward thinking, and improvement focused. Work together to come up with strategies that will work best for their individual position, skill set, and interests. While going through this process, allow for differences. People can serve the organization and realize their full potential in different ways. Below are some steps for creating that dialogue:

- Step 1: Ask questions that help them identify what they want to do, how they want to do it, and how they want to be held accountable in ways that will help them achieve those goals.

- Step 2: Provide some pushback. Negotiate to set goals that push team members further than they think they can go but not further than they actually can.
- Step 3: Explore possible consequences. What will those goals yield? Are they sustainable? Will they have desirable impact that benefits others, the reviewee, and the organization?

To overcome the threat of bias in performance reviews, bear less responsibility. To avoid imposing your culturally relative criteria on others, invite them to articulate more of their own. Require them to explain how those parameters meet the organization's goals and their job duties. Set parameters that are not only narrow enough to achieve coordinated organizational targets but also broad enough for people to personalize them. Collaboration doesn't mean carte blanche. It is a negotiation between the needs of the company and the wants of the individual. Push but also bend. Yield in ways that inspire initiative, and assert in ways that stimulate conviction. Instead of setting uniform targets and expecting everyone to accept them, practice inclusivity by creating a structure where people can identify goals that are best both for them and for the organization.

10. INCREASE TRANSPARENCY.

Distrust undermines performance reviews. Employees will resist them if they don't understand them. Team members will grudgingly and insincerely comply if they expect appraisals are meaningless. If people suspect the process is biased, productivity will drop. Those who benefit from bias will coast, and those who suffer from it will cave.

To overcome all these issues, make your review process more transparent. High-trust organizations outperform their counterparts by 286 percent in total returns. To make your process more trustworthy, articulate the process in thorough detail. Publish the criteria, numerical assignments, rubrics, explanations, and fictional examples of evidence. Post results of the norming sessions that use fictional profiles so reviewees can see what kinds of performances receive what kinds of reviews. Make sure employees know where this information is. Offer regular trainings to help team members understand what to expect. Beyond detailing steps, provide rationale for why the process is how it is. Hold town hall meetings so people can discuss the criteria and ask questions.

The point of performance reviews is to improve performance. Therefore, provide everyone with the tools they need to do that. There is no "cheat sheet," because appraisals aren't a pop quiz. To earn trust, examine the process, and invite scrutiny. Have answers and be open to questions. Involve people in the process and prepare to modify things according to their findings. Whatever you do, minimize anxiety and maximize quality by being transparent about performance reviews.

11. DECENTRALIZE DECISIONS.

Circumvent the prejudices that disproportionately harm people from underrepresented groups by building in processes that decentralize decisions. Reviewers can have biases that drive them to impose their goals on others, so make goal setting a collaborative process between reviewers and reviewees. Infrequent reviews magnify the impact of each, so restructure the process. Move from deciding the professional futures of people based on a few high-stakes review sessions, and start basing them on the culmination of many low-stakes ones.

Also decentralize decisions between one reviewer and multiple reviewers. Answer the problem of idiosyncratic rater effect with inter-rater reliability. John can give Nicole a bad review because Nicole deserves one, but he could also give her a bad review because he doesn't like her. To see if a review is a reflection of Nicole or a projection of John, build in a review cycle where Nicole is also reviewed by Tim. Try creating review committees and averaging scores according to multiple or independent reviews. If this sounds like too much work, send reviews to committees randomly, like a spot check for quality control. If you're worried about personality clashes between reviewers, consider setting up a process where the identities of multiple reviewers remain anonymous.

Of course, organizations have different resources and will be able to accomplish this kind of decentralization to different degrees. In each situation, however, the point is to remember that the current review process disadvantages people from underrepresented groups. To undo this unfairness in particular and improve the entire process in general, recognize how much weight this decision deserves and find ways to ensure it's carried by multiple people to lower the chances that bias creeps in.

12. PROPOSE 360-DEGREE REVIEWS.

If you encounter people who insist the standard review process is acceptable, nothing will get them to improve it like subjecting them to it. I'm always fascinated to hear managers refute suggestions for improving this process. When we review data about bias, they'll expend a vast amount of mental energy insisting the process is fair . . . until I recommend they go through it. In my experience, few things motivate improvements to reviews like approaching superiors and proposing that the organization seek 360-degree feedback, having every member of the organization receive evaluations by their supervisors, colleagues, and subordinates.

Forced to comply with the whims, ambiguity, and dread of the void, even reluctant leaders who cling to the status quo suddenly become prolific innovators open to all kinds of new ways to revitalize the review process. If their pay and promotion gets tied to what their subordinates have to say about them, suddenly they become the best champions for change. For this reason, if you want to discover the flaws of your review process, go through it. If you truly want to see how it affects your team members, have them evaluate you. If you're serious about making your performance reviews more inclusive, build a bridge and be the first to walk across it.

"Answers from the Void"

Many businesses use hiring to achieve diversity. Some companies go further and improve internal practices to create greater equity. But the organizations that are most inclusive are those that have marginalized communities represented at higher levels of authority. They ensure that people with underrepresented perspectives from underrepresented groups have opportunities to advance into positions of leadership where they can put those perspectives into action.

The key to the advancement that makes all this possible is a mountain resting on a pebble, and that pebble is the performance review process. It becomes the pinch point that can block or unleash all the potential of an organization's DEI strategy. Critics claim inclusivity is reverse discrimination, using unfair quotas to promote unqualified minorities. Some people agree with the principles of DEI but fear making drastic changes to their infrastructure. But this chapter has shown that you can achieve greater fairness for all with a few minor but strategic adjustments to the performance review process.

Without inspiring backlash or undergoing a complete overhaul, organizations can open possibilities by making a few key changes. While these alterations might seem like insignificant tweaks to the performance review form, process, and structure, they often prove to be the deciding factor in whether an organization achieves more inclusion at higher levels of leadership. While holding norming sessions, making goals collaborative, and scaffolding reviews might not seem earth shattering, they are. Just ask all the Jasons on your team. There are few things more groundbreaking than finding ways to get answers from the void.

CHAPTER ELEVEN

Next Steps
Personalizing Your DEI Approach

On a Friday afternoon, I delivered a presentation on inclusion for a company I'll call Frequent Inc. Hundreds of employees filled my computer screen to hear strategies for cultivating workplace belonging. But among the crowd, it didn't take long for me to notice someone whom I'll call Paul. He joined the meeting three minutes late, cleared his throat into the microphone until I muted him, then assumed all the nonverbals of a classic resistant audience member. Before long, the other members of the audience faded from my view. All I could see was Paul sitting there smirking with his arms crossed. Despite all the stories I told, statistics I provided, and jokes I cracked, he sat there unpersuaded.

As the powers of technology whisked hundreds away to share their ideas in breakout rooms, I imagined Paul unleashing the diatribe he had been amassing. Alone with his peers, he was enlisting others to his cause, and when we came back for group discussion, he would lead the charge against me that would contradict all the training I'd delivered that day, roll back all the DEI objectives Frequent Inc. had articulated over the previous few months, and undo all the civil rights advances the United States had achieved in its almost 250-year history!

Before long, the main meeting room began to repopulate with participants fresh from their discussion. As a wave of pixelated rectangles returned, there sat Paul. When I took a deep breath and asked who would like to share with the group, the first to use the Raise Hand function was Paul. Here it had come, the moment I feared, and there was nothing to do but mutter a prayer and apologize for the part I had played in what was about to happen.

"Yes, Paul. How can you improve inclusion at Frequent Inc.?" And what followed did embarrass me. But his response didn't humiliate me with a tirade defending the status quo. Instead, his answer humbled me because of how practical, thoughtful, and personal it was. "I liked the idea of the round-robin," he said. "With my team, I'm going to start making sure nobody talks twice till everyone gets a chance to speak once. That one stuck with me."

CEOs issue public statements, their direct subordinates deliver mandates, and then trainers deliver lectures, but effective DEI always requires room for the audiences to process, respond, and talk back. I've taken years scouting the information for this book, but readers must take the lessons from my experience and filter them through their own experiences.

With initiatives in organizations, learning opportunities in a training, or even when engaging with a book, DEI becomes its best when it encourages people to move beyond being passive receivers of information and become active creators of it.

That is the invitation I leave you with—to not only take the tips from these pages and translate them to your own situation but also add to them. To create inclusivity, learn what has worked for many organizations and personalize it. DEI objectives work best when we move from monologue to dialogue and clear a space for that terrifying and chaotic but essential moment when people have the chance to independently say, "That one stuck with me."

The first part of this book focused on personal development, finding ways to use your privilege to benefit others, check yourself and diversify your business thinking, and build a bridge with financial and moral arguments for DEI. The second part concentrated on organizational improvement, looking at recruiting, hiring, onboarding, retention, mentoring, meetings, and performance reviews. To conclude, we must examine how to tailor these tips to your unique situation. To ensure that reading *Actions Speak Louder* turns into action, here are some ways to modify them for your organization.

Steps for Action

1. CONDUCT AN AUDIT.

This book covers best practices that have worked at many organizations, but there might be other strategies that are even better for your own. Before charging into the fray, do the research. Fight the temptation to assume you know the problems, and leave open the possibility that you can still learn, even about an organization you are so close to. In combating workplace bias, don't fall into biases about your own workplace. Remain curious enough to learn and challenge your assumptions. Survey people. Ask them what they want to learn regarding DEI. Inquire about problems they've experienced. Solicit advice regarding areas for improvement and greater inclusivity. Survey business partners, vendors, clients, customers, consumers, and community partners with questions about how the company can foster deeper belonging. Analyze core documents to identify a "constitution" for the organization. Specify goals that are most relevant to your particular company. Define the most pertinent measurements for gauging progress. Avoid the temptation to assume one size fits all. Find out what makes the most sense for your organization. Hire consultants to provide outside expertise and perspective and firm nudges in a forward direction.

2. MAKE SCHEDULES.

Create commitments far in advance. Devise the goals you have for three years from now, then work backward. Break those up into the annual benchmarks you would have to complete. Spend extra attention on the targets you would have to accomplish by the end of this year. Then break those up into months. Divide those objectives into time slots and create a regular rotation of meetings that would set the organization up for success. Ensure all scheduled tasks lead to the next. Align organizational, departmental, and individual goals. Translate annual reports into quarterly reports, performance reviews, and frequent meetings. Do whatever you can from a scheduling standpoint to ensure all tasks feed into these larger goals. By tying these objectives into the tasks people are already doing, you'll minimize resistance and exhaustion while maximizing efficiency. But put a year's worth of meetings on the books as soon as possible. Few things will motivate people to stay on task like knowing they have a regular set of meetings coming up every first Thursday of the month, every other Wednesday, or every Tuesday.

3. CONTINUE LEARNING.

Identify areas for educational development. Refer to your audit for guidance. Rather than delving into topics you find interesting, base DEI training for your team on survey results. Balance what people want to learn with things the evidence suggests they need to learn. In addition to having one ninety-minute training session, have frequent refresher exercises. Combine the opportunity to learn about concepts with educational presentations like activities, workshops, and application work that help people practice putting these lessons into action. As much as possible, specialize training to the specific tasks for specific people. For example, in addition to the hour-long keynote on bias to your entire organization, have opportunities for hiring managers to practice mitigating bias in the hiring process or for executives to have training on how to circumvent bias in intercultural mentorships. Whatever the case, find ways to make the training as accessible and relevant as possible.

4. BUILD COMMITTEES.

No one can do this work on their own, and no one should. Get help from others. Create a committee where members have the opportunity to inspire one another. Surround yourself with committee members who will keep you in check. When picking them, make sure you keep the following considerations in mind. Gather people humble enough to recognize their biases yet bold enough to call you on yours. Draw folks from different ethnicities, genders, sexual orientations, ability statuses, religions, nationalities, language backgrounds, ages, and military statuses. Assemble wide representation from different departments within your organization. Bring together participants from different levels in the organization from the C-suite to the custodial staff as well as everyone from board members to community members.

Support the committee with funding, release time, and advancement opportunities. Be strategic about planning logistics to alleviate all burdens. While creating a situation where committee members can center DEI, find ways to tweak everyday things so everyone is involved. Ideally, the DEI committee does strategic planning, but the work is carried out by everyone. Committees are important for providing oversight, but don't let everyone else relegate it to them.

5. CREATE ACCOUNTABILITY.

Specify the objectives the committee is supposed to achieve, the scope of their investigation, and the reach of their power. Spend lots of time getting explicit agreement from leadership on not only what they are willing to let the committee do but also what they're willing to submit to. Toward the beginning of your process, create structures for critique that question and improve their objectives and practices. Design opportunities for honest critique through tailored meetings, reporting structures, and anonymous surveys that invite true candor.

Beyond these conversations between the committee and leaders, increase chances for organizational change by engaging your community. People are more likely to achieve goals if they make themselves accountable for doing so. Achieve this kind of external accountability by publishing your DEI goals, plans, and reports. If you are a publicly traded company, use this material as part of the extended narrative already required for your Form 10-Ks, ESG reports, and human capital reporting. If you're a nonprofit or governmental organization, these publications can serve to help you report to your community what you're doing to fulfill your mission, vision, and values. If you're a privately owned company, they can be valuable documents for showing customers, consumers, clients, current workers, and prospective employees how you're planning to achieve the inclusivity that these stakeholders want. Whatever you do, increase the prospect that you'll achieve your goals by looking to outside parties that will hold you accountable.

6. ASSESS.

While there are many steps that apply to most organizations, remember to do the work of individualizing DEI to your organization. The most successful leaders modify general principles to their particular organization, considering how much their team can financially, philosophically, and logistically support DEI. Identifying both proponents and opponents of it, as well as the reluctant people in between, they discover obstacles and evaluate their company's capacity for change. While eager to improve, they appreciate the comfort level of others. To make up for these restrictions, they spend time determining the unique skills of individuals and how those skills will advance initiatives. They seek support from executives, board members, clients, organizational partners, and community members. While striving to push people beyond their comfort zone, they also try to see people's limits when it comes to time, skill, and temperament.

7. REASSESS.

Those who are most successful are those who relentlessly find the silver lining in every cloud. They recognize their limitations and find some way to flip them into strengths. Using solutions-oriented thinking, creative problem solving, and ingenuity, they work around restrictions and devise ways to achieve DEI goals without the resources most think are necessary. If they have no financial support, they look for grants, external partnerships, and outside funding. Others have a task force of introverts, so they give them chances to express opinions through writing, planning, and restructuring behind the scenes. I coach plenty of DEI innovators who work in organizations that won't give them a dime, so they've assembled a team of volunteers willing to pilot DEI initiatives without any funding in order to research the successes of these groups in comparison to others. Whatever your situation, find ways to flip every obstacle into an opportunity.

8. ASSESS YOURSELF.

One of the things I find most exciting about DEI work is how the quest for greater inclusion can be so inclusive. While striving to help organizations become more welcoming to people of all kinds of social identities, the DEI movement also becomes more welcoming to people with all kinds of personalities and skills. Some are drawn to training, while others look at policy. There are those who can persuade opponents, and there are those who are so diplomatic they never seem to draw any foes. The point is that there are many different ways to do this work, and one of my greatest honors has been seeing all the creative things others have done to ensure the greatest number of people can show up as their whole selves for the greatest good. Part of achieving that noble task is figuring out how you can show up as your most authentic self in this DEI work. My goal in writing this book is to gather dots and invite you to connect them in ways that make the most sense to you.

Be honest about what you can and can't do. Take a deep look at your skills and assets. Be real about your authority level in your organization, but understand how to be resourceful enough to find ways to make changes without an official title. Be honest about your personality type, taking stock of which assets to capitalize on and which liabilities to manage. Learn how to balance the courage it takes to propose these changes as well as the humility required to know how to ask for help. Take the time to craft thoughtful plans, but also know when to improvise. Ask yourself:

- What authority do I have in my organization?
- Even if I don't have formal titles, what kind of informal influence do I have?
- What is my personality type? What is it not?
- What tasks fit well with that personality?
- What tasks would be better delegated to others?

If your self-assessment revealed limitations, turn them into possibilities. If you're an entry-level employee who has no institutional authority, use your beginner's status as an opportunity to ask a lot of questions without seeming rude or interrogative. Reference your experience at previous companies to help members within their current business get a peek at what their competitors are already doing in DEI. If you're embarrassed by your inability to win arguments, draw on your organizational skills and attention to detail. If you can't make arguments on the fly, build cases slowly, methodically, and thoroughly.

9. BUILD ON YOUR COMPETENCIES.

If you're going to use your privilege to benefit others, you must find ways to build on the competencies you already possess. The way to build bridges is to focus on the unique knowledge, experience, and skills that you have that can serve others. DEI presents opportunities to learn, grow, and reach, but there's plenty of room for difference. One thing might work for others, but something else might work for you. The strategies laid out in this book might present valuable paths, but you will also have your own course to chart.

10. INTEGRATE DEI INTO YOUR CURRENT TASKS.

In addition to building on the competencies you already have, find ways to incorporate DEI into the tasks you're already doing. In "Managing the Toll of DEI Work: The Physiology of Inclusion," Kevin Carter, principal strategist with the Winters Group, claims DEI supporters need to balance their desire to serve with their need for self-care. Advocates and allies are willing to sacrifice, but they must avoid exhaustion so that sacrifice benefits others. Essential to that objective is avoiding the tendency to add on and burn out. Instead, you must look at the tasks you're already doing and ask how you can feed many birds from one fountain. Instead of assuming you must create entirely new tasks, ask how you can tweak old ones.

Some resist this line of thought, suspecting that self-care is synonymous with selfishness, but statistics show it is also tied to long-term effectiveness. In "How to Get Middle Managers to Commit to D&I," human resources writer Katie Clarey notes that drastic changes from the top down rarely work. She points out that effective DEI programs are those that seem less like an outside imposition and instead seek to foster internal motivation. Crucial to this goal is to stop thinking about inclusivity as something special and start thinking about it as something essential. Instead of being something we add on to our job, it must become something we integrate into our job. Therefore, you have to find ways to see DEI potential in where people already are and in what they're already doing. For some that may seem like taking the "easy way out," but statistics show this integrative approach is fundamental to achieving sustainability.

11. BE AUTHENTIC.

Beyond competencies and tasks, build on your interests. DEI work requires extraordinary diplomacy and adaptability. Creating consensus all the time can be exhausting and lead to feelings of inauthenticity. To avoid being performative, one of the things you have to do is be honest about who you are and who you aren't. Take inventory of your interests. In DEI, those who stand out the most are those who are interested in politics, social issues, and cultural change. But if you're interested in something else, don't ignore those interests. If you're passionate about food, explore what DEI could look like through potlucks. If your hobby is the arts, be creative about how you could advance inclusivity through painting. If your calling in life is accounting, think deeply about how financial systems could help foster greater belonging.

Be honest about what makes you curious. No matter how seemingly strange, insignificant, or obscure those interests might be, confess them. You might find them weird, silly, or embarrassing, but they could also be the key to the particular version of DEI that works best for you. Who knows, the unique combination of your interests and the principles provided here might be the key to unlocking a variety of inclusivity the world has never seen. The organizations that become more inclusive are the ones that allow people to incorporate greater inclusivity into who they already are. They build on people's preexisting competencies, tasks, and interests.

Make It Personal

In the story about DEI training that began this chapter, I was terrified to give the floor to Paul. The second I handed over the microphone, I couldn't control what he would say. I ran the risk of my presentation going off the rails. While his comment didn't undermine the virtues of inclusivity, I was hoping conversation would be more groundbreaking. Building on Paul's initial comment, the rest of the discussion time focused on meeting dynamics and after-work activities that could help people get along more. The conclusion of this meeting wasn't as bad as I thought it was going to be, but it wasn't as good as I'd hoped. Where was the insightful conversation about performance reviews? What about statistics regarding gender disparities in mentoring? After I pressed the button to end the virtual meeting, I spent the rest of the afternoon upset with myself that I hadn't crafted a presentation that did a better job of inspiring profound conversation.

But months later, the organization Paul works for has made profound changes. Over a multiyear process, they've performed the kind of deep dive into thinking, decision-making, practice, and operations that transform companies. The leaders of Paul's organization were anticipating strong resistance to their DEI initiatives. To their surprise, they found enthusiastic participation. In their deeper research, they found that a key element of their success was the fact that team members of that organization had room to personalize DEI. Rather than being something done to them, it became something they could do. Instead of being something imposed upon them, inclusivity became something they could help create in ways that made sense to them. For some, that means overhauling their hiring strategies. For others, it means investing fortunes into a mentorship program. For Paul, it was starting with how he held meetings. Most of the time, the things that resonate the most are the little acts of micro-inclusion that participants have control over and can implement immediately.

DEI is a beautiful practice that combines form and function. In advocating for diversity, it also advocates for a diversity of strategies. In striving for greater equity, it recognizes the need for equitable approaches to this work. In venerating inclusivity, it clears space to include more people in the conversation. Practicing DEI deconstructs monologue into dialogue. You'll turn dialogue into a conversation full of many perspectives. Give the ignored a platform to speak. Instead of speaking for them, listen until they find their voice. Rather than dominate the space with all the things you have to say, leave room for others to find what sticks with them.

Actions Speak Louder

The new hope I felt during the summer of 2020 came from the sense that people were ready to do more. My great-great-grandfather never received justice. My uncle Buck never wanted to talk about his tragedy at all. But leaders seem to have emerged who are willing to do the work that so many generations have neglected. They appear ready to recognize the role that business has in creating fairness where other social institutions fail. Beyond leaving it to public officials to correct wrongs, they look ready to explore how modifications to recruiting, hiring, onboarding, retention, mentoring, meetings, and performance reviews can make things right. In addition to speaking out against injustice, they seem ready to create the economic conditions that avoid injustice in the first place.

At the same time, the social changes that can come through organizational improvement require your personal assessment. They demand that those so eager to speak out are also willing to act out by looking inward. Many allies charge ahead, focusing so deeply on structural problems that they overlook the personality problems that undermine their efforts. But inclusive leaders realize that to change practices, procedures, and policies, they must also change themselves. They must ask the hard questions.

- How can I implement DEI?
- What does my DEI self-assessment look like?
- How can I reassess myself in ways that turn obstacles into opportunities?
- How can I build on my preexisting competencies to integrate DEI most confidently?
- How can I incorporate DEI into the tasks I already do so I can integrate DEI most sustainably?
- How can I build on my preexisting interests so I can integrate DEI most authentically?
- Who am I?
- How would my most authentic DEI work look?

Whatever your answers to these questions, never stop asking them. From this book, use what works. Add to it where it leaves gaps. Whatever you do, be the new hope the world is looking for. Break the silence to speak up, but as you seek your particular DEI approach in those words, always remember actions speak louder.

Additional Support

would love to hear how you implement these tips and devise your own. One of the most exciting things about teaching what I've learned is that sharing this information creates opportunities for me to keep learning from others. Let me know your findings and your failures, your experiments and your discoveries. There are still answers to be found, still new ways to create inclusivity, still deeper methods for fostering belonging. Let's build on the experiences together. If you've read this book and are looking for ways to personalize your DEI approach, and want some support along the way, connect with us at www.upliftingimpact.com/actions-speak-louder or actions@upliftingimpact.com. There you will find additional resources and information on how to work with us directly.

Acknowledgments

My heart is overflowing with gratitude. I am confident the ink on this paper will not do justice to how much I appreciate the people who helped to make this happen, and I know that I can't list you all. If you helped shape this book in any way, and are not listed here, please know that I am deeply grateful and charge my omission to my mind and not my heart.

First, to the team at Uplifting Impact. You all inspire me every day with your commitment to building bridges and helping others. Your willingness to bring your talents and passions to our work is humbling. I am honored to serve with you.

To the Uplifting Impact clients, the leaders, and organizations, thank you for having the courage to take action and build a more inclusive world.

To the students in the Professional Certificate in Diversity, Equity, and Inclusion program at the University of Wisconsin–Madison, thank you for the joy of teaching and learning from you all. You will see yourselves within these pages.

To Mark and Kristi Westover, I will never forget your kindness and how you opened up your home to me so I could write the first draft. Thank you for being such great friends.

To Kate Leibfried, you are an immensely talented writing coach, and I appreciate the fact that you kept me moving every time I wanted to give up.

To Jessica Faust, you are an amazing agent, and sometimes I pinch myself when I think about how lucky I am that we found each other. Thanks for being my guide.

To the Penguin Random House team. Thank you for believing in me and inviting me to share this book through your platform. I especially want to thank Regina Andreoni, Lillian Ball, and my amazing editors, Kimberly Meilun and Leah Trouwborst. I appreciate your commitment to the work and your ability to manage me so well!

To my sisters, Ranjit Singh and Kulbir Singh, who cheered for me and made me stop and celebrate along the way.

To my parents, Bachan Singh and Patricia Singh, you are my favorite bridge builders.

To my children, Zion Singh Ponder and Zephaniah Singh Ponder, my greatest hope is that the world you and future generations inherit is better because of this book.

Justin Ponder, you are my favorite person in the whole world. Without you, this book would not be real. Thank you for waking up in the middle of the night to help me with editing. Thank you for listening to me as I worked through ideas. Thank you for letting me live life by your side.

Appendix A

Part I Exercises

The first three chapters have exercises for personal reflection. They appear here in condensed format for easier reference.

Chapter One: "Dinner Table" Exercise

1. Make two columns.
2. Title one "Porcelain."
3. Title other "Thali."
4. In the Porcelain column, list all your workplace privileges.
5. In the Thali column, flip each of your workplace privileges into things you can do to benefit others.

QUESTIONS TO CONSIDER:

1. What other workplace privileges do you have?
2. How can you use them to benefit others?

3. What workplace privileges do you have that might be actively disadvantaging others?

4. How can you spread that privilege around so it doesn't harm others?

5. One problem with allyship is saviorism. Some begin to assume that they hold the power, knowledge, or skill to save, and that those who need saving are powerless, ignorant, and useless. What steps can you take to ensure you're using your privilege to benefit others without falling into the traps of saviorism?

Chapter Two: "Green Rabbits Graph" Exercise

1. Make three columns.

2. Title the middle column "Unprofessionalism."

3. In that middle column, list all the things that are obviously "unprofessional."

4. In the left column, write "Bias."

5. In that left column, note which social group is privileged by each characteristic listed in the Unprofessionalism column.

6. Cross out the Unprofessionalism title.

7. Replace it with the title "White Bears."

8. Title the right column "Green Rabbits."

9. For each characteristic written in the White Bears column, go to the Green Rabbits column and write a benefit.

QUESTIONS TO CONSIDER:

1. While this exercise focuses on definitions of professionalism, what other workplace biases exist?

2. How can you substitute them with diversified business thinking?

3. This exercise concentrates on helping you challenge your workplace biases. Beyond being a conceptual exercise that broadens your perception, what practical actions might your findings suggest?

4. For each of the benefits you listed in the Green Rabbits column, what could be the organizational impact?

5. This exercise focuses on your individual perception of an individual's actions, but we must consider larger team dynamics. How might each item listed in the Green Rabbits column affect other team members? What steps must you take to minimize the problems and maximize the benefits each green rabbit can have on others?

Chapter Three: "Build a Bridge" Exercise

1. Get a poster board.

2. Title it "Bridge."

3. Make four columns with plenty of space between them.

4. Title the second column "Opposition to DEI."

5. In it, list all the reasons you have heard or can imagine hearing that oppose workplace DEI.

6. Title the first column "Value."

7. Take each argument that appears in the second column and write in the first column the corresponding value that drives that argument (financial or moral).

8. Title the third column "Evidence."

9. In it, write evidence that addresses counterarguments driven by business values.

10. Research your organization's mission, vision, and values statements. Track down the employee handbook, HR materials, policies, and public declarations. They are your organization's "constitution."

11. In the third column, use this information to write evidence that addresses counterarguments driven by moral values.

12. Title the fourth column "Proposal."

13. While you are reading this book, when you come across a strategy you want to consider for your organization, write it in the Proposal column. Create a clear bridge from one supporting beam to the next, linking the proposed strategy to the evidence, opposition, and value columns that precede it.

14. Use this bridge as the foundation for all the other technical chapters that follow. Before implementing a policy to change recruiting, hiring, onboarding, retention, mentoring, meetings, and performance reviews, tie each back to a core value of the organization.

QUESTIONS TO CONSIDER:

1. This exercise concentrates on financial and moral arguments. Which other kinds of arguments do people use to resist DEI? What evidence can you use to address those concerns and earn support?

2. Even if you convince people to conceptually agree with DEI initiatives, what other forms of resistance might you experience? How can procrastination, lack of money, or insufficient

staffing undermine DEI? What tactics can you use to turn these forms of passive resistance into support?

3. This bridge-building exercise creates the structure for presenting proposals to stakeholders, but what if you don't have access to the most powerful stakeholders in your organization? To whom do you have access? Do you have access to the people who have access? Even if you don't have the influence to make decisions, how can these proposals influence the decision makers?

4. What groups or handful of people can you work with in your organization to amplify these proposals?

5. For each of the chapters that follow, which tips will you use? How can you create a bridge between a new initiative and one of the organization's core values?

Appendix B

Part II Discussion Guide: Questions to Apply to Your Particular Experience and Organization

This book has surveyed best practices, academic studies, and many of my own experiences in the DEI space. The following provides opportunities for you to do some personal reflection and tailor these recommendations to your own experiences, thinking about what would work best for your skill set, your situation, and your particular organization.

Chapter Four: Recruiting

1. **Multiply the number of people who write your job advertisements.**
   a. How many people will be enough to write your job advertisements?
   b. Which departments will they come from, and how many levels of leadership will they represent?
   c. How can this process support and not undermine the people who normally write job advertisements?

2. **Diversify the backgrounds of job advertisement writers.**

    a. What steps can diversify the backgrounds of these writers?

    b. What procedures can determine the backgrounds necessary depending on the job?

    c. What precautions can gain the perspectives of people from different backgrounds without exhausting the same handful of people from underrepresented groups?

3. **Remove biased language.**

    a. If the job advertisements were also an advertisement for your organization, what do they say about your organization's values?

    b. According to their focus, tone, words, and references, what values do they imply?

    c. Beyond words that are explicitly racist, sexist, homophobic, transphobic, classist, ableist, or ageist, what other biased language does your job advertisement have?

    d. Each text is written with an ideal reader in mind. Read your job advertisements. Who is its implied reader? What is that reader's race, gender, sexual orientation, socioeconomic class, ability status, and age? How does that coincide with the goals of the job advertisement?

    e. After biased language has been removed, what kind of language does the job advertisement add to prove it represents an inclusive organization?

4. **Revise titles.**

    a. What titles does your job advertisement use?

    b. What are the historical, cultural, and social implications of those titles? What do they mean for people from different groups?

    c. How will these titles affect the ability to attract applicants from various backgrounds?

5. **Reconsider unnecessary comparisons.**

    a. What comparisons does your job advertisement make? How often does it use words that end in "-er" or "-est"?

    b. What is the purpose of these comparisons? Are they necessary? Why?

    c. How might they affect the ability to attract applicants from underrepresented communities?

6. **Shorten lists of qualifications.**

    a. How many qualifications does your job advertisement list? Why?

    b. Do they represent a wish list of desired qualifications or required ones?

    c. Which can be trimmed away? Why? How will this trimming affect the kinds of applicants the ad will attract?

7. **Use recruitment techniques that centralize underrepresented communities.**

    a. What are your current recruitment strategies?

    b. Where do you recruit? What groups dominate those places? When recruiting there, what kinds of applicants do you usually get?

    c. What groups do you want to reach? Where are they? What platforms do they gravitate toward? How can they be reached through them?

8. **Prove you actually support those communities.**

    a. What is the plan to develop relationships with platforms that reach these communities?

    b. What can the organization do to be authentic enough to stand out from all the other organizations doing the same thing?

    c. How can you prove you're not a "poacher" who's just looking to get some quick diversity numbers before ignoring and demoralizing the people these platforms serve?

9. **Articulate your organization's DEI brand.**

   a. What is your organization's DEI brand? Why is your organization committed to DEI? What has it done to prove its commitment to DEI?

   b. What does your organization offer that others don't? Why should people from underrepresented groups join it as opposed to the many others that espouse DEI values?

   c. What proof exists that would make marginalized people think your organization would be a place where they are welcome?

10. **Rethink your current networks.**

    a. What are the underrepresented groups you want to recruit from? Why? How would this recruitment benefit the recruit? How would it benefit the underrepresented group they come from?

    b. What connections does your organization already have with those groups? What ERGs, affinity groups, internship programs, mentorship programs, and community partnerships do you already have with those groups? What employees have ties to those social groups?

    c. What strategies can reach out to your existing network of people from underrepresented groups in ways that are authentic? People who run ERGs, affinity groups, internship programs, mentorship programs, and community partnerships are often doing this work voluntarily; how can you reach out to them for networking in ways that make their life easier instead of harder? How can you reach out to employees for referrals to their communities in ways that are authentic, respectful, mutually advantageous, and dignified without being exploitative or opportunistic?

11. **Miscellaneous**

    a. What other things can make your recruitment process more inclusive?

b. What obstacles do you anticipate? What strategies can solve those problems?

c. If you do not have the authority to implement these recruiting strategies, how can you propose changes to the people who do?

d. When it comes to DEI recruiting, what volunteer opportunities could you offer for yourself or a DEI committee?

e. What data would you have to collect to demonstrate the effectiveness of this program? How would you collect that data?

Chapter Five: Hiring

1. **Redact résumés.**

   a. What skills are essential to fulfill the advertised job?

   b. What skills are not?

   c. What questions are essential to assessing how qualified candidates are for the advertised job?

2. **Specify criteria.**

   a. Beyond the qualifications listed on a job advertisement, what criteria are used to decide which résumés advance?

   b. Who decided those criteria? How?

   c. What committee can improve these criteria? How does this committee represent differing perspectives? How can they become more inclusive? What rationale exists to prove these revised criteria will improve the organization?

3. **Consider questionnaires.**

   a. While much of the information that goes into an application might not be essential to assessing a candidate's qualifications, a lot of that information remains important. How can questionnaires collect important information from applicants in a different place than the qualifications that résumé reviewers assess?

    b. What kind of information do people usually provide in the résumés, cover letters, and other application materials they submit to your organization? To collect this information, what questions would a questionnaire ask?

    c. This process is unusual for many organizations. What points would convince hiring personnel that these changes will make their job easier, more focused, and more efficient?

4. Hire for "culture add."

    a. During your organization's hiring process, what are the specific things that are said or done that show people have fallen back into hiring for culture fit?

    b. What are the homogeneities of your organization and the shortcomings they create?

    c. What are criteria for culture add that you'd like to see?

    d. What points would convince people to hire for culture add?

    e. What changes would get people enthusiastic about hiring for culture add? What would make this process as easy as possible for those who must enthusiastically support it for it to succeed?

5. Restructure interviewing to require culture add.

    a. What kinds of questions would make interviewees demonstrate how they would add to organizational culture?

    b. This practice can be unusual. What can encourage interviewees to engage with it honestly and not suspect they're being lured into a trap?

    c. What scoring structures can ensure hirers reward interviewees for demonstrating their ability to add to the organizational culture and not punish them for failing to fit into it?

6. **Think creatively about anonymizing interviews.**

   a. At your organization, how would written responses work for particular kinds of interviews? What kinds of questions should be asked? What kinds of project-based and problem-solving scenarios could be included?

   b. While many of these strategies restructure interviews to restrict information in ways that circumvent bias, what training can help interviewers manage their bias so they can conduct face-to-face interviews?

   c. What are the virtues of face-to-face interviews? What are their risks? What are the virtues of redacted interviews? What are their drawbacks? Given answers to these questions, what is the best option for your organization when it comes to interviewing for a particular position?

7. **Make the selection process transparent.**

   a. When did the organization identify the need for the new position? Why?

   b. How did the job description form? Who formed it?

   c. Was there a hiring committee? Why or why not? Who was on it? How was it decided who would be on it? Who was responsible for what?

   d. How was the job advertisement drafted and why? Where was it posted and why?

   e. Being as specific as possible, which criteria were used to identify the résumés that would receive callbacks?

   f. What steps were made to manage the biases inherent in the résumé-review process?

   g. Which criteria were used to identify which interviewees would advance? How were interviews conducted? Given all the ways bias can undermine the interview process, what steps were taken to remain fair? How were interviewees assessed?

   h. How was the final selection decided? Who made the decision? How? Why that person or those people?

8. **Provide better messaging.**

   a. Before the new team member starts their first day, what kind of messaging can explain the hiring decision and demonstrate the new hire's credentials?

   b. What information can be legally, ethically, and diplomatically shared in ways that obey the law, retain the dignity of the new hire, and not stir the animosity of other team members?

   c. What information should remain private and confidential?

Chapter Six: Onboarding

1. **Change your philosophical approach to onboarding.**

   a. According to most people at your organization, what's the purpose of onboarding?

   b. How does your organization's current approach emphasize assimilation?

   c. What difficulties would arise if you encouraged people to challenge this approach?

2. **Create an onboarding team.**

   a. What would be the charge of your onboarding team? What metrics would you use to measure its success? How would you collect data?

   b. How would you decide whom you'd ask to join the onboarding team? Why?

   c. How would you ensure the onboarding team was willing, able, and not exhausted?

3. **Ensure the onboarding team is diverse.**

   a. What kind of diversity does your particular onboarding team need? For what specific purposes?

b. Besides diversity of social identity, what kind of representation do you need from multiple departments and organizational levels on this team?

c. How many people do you need on your onboarding team? What tasks will each do? For how long?

4. Send the onboarding team through DEI training.

a. What specific DEI onboarding needs does your organization have? What specific training can meet those needs?

b. Trainers will provide background that surveys best practices across multiple organizations. How can you also conduct research to pinpoint the specific onboarding challenges and opportunities at your particular organization?

c. As part of this training, the team should clarify its purpose. What are its onboarding goals, DEI values, and possible complications? What are its shared terms, goals, and tactics?

5. Review onboarding paperwork.

a. What paperwork gets circulated during the onboarding process?

b. What does that information explicitly state about the organization's commitment to DEI? What does it imply?

c. What does that information say about the opportunities people from underrepresented groups might have to grow, report problems, and provide differing points of view?

6. Include all identity options.

a. Where are the many points where new hires complete forms? Do all those forms have inclusive identifiers that represent all identities?

b. What would it take for all those forms to move from providing options for people to select from and start allowing respondents to fill in blanks?

c. What logistical considerations would this change entail? What software changes would it require? How would it alter the data your organization has collected and the information it has?

7. Consider community connections.

a. How can the onboarding process be improved to introduce new hires to associations, events, and places in the community?

b. How can you structure pre-onboarding conversations to learn more about new hires and the kinds of community connections that might be appropriate for them?

8. Create a pre-onboarding stage.

a. What compliance items can become part of the pre-onboarding stage?

b. What information can new hires cover electronically through email or videos?

c. What activities can help new hires make personal connections in their first week?

d. What kinds of scheduling can ensure they make connections with people at different levels of the organization (other new hires, team members, and supervisors)?

9. Involve new hires in planning their welcoming activities.

a. What kind of questionnaire, informal conversations, or "get-to-know-me" exercises can you schedule to learn more about new hires before their onboarding even begins?

b. What questions can personalize the onboarding experience for new hires?

c. What else can make people feel included in their own onboarding experience?

10. **Include diverse perspectives.**

    a. What diverse perspectives would be important for your onboarding experience?

    b. What process can ensure the people you invite to give these perspectives will be beneficial for the new team members going through onboarding?

    c. What steps will increase the likelihood of their willingness to provide these perspectives?

11. **Invite ERG leaders.**

    a. What pre-onboarding "get-to-know-me" exercises can determine which ERG leaders new hires would like to meet?

    b. What can be done to avoid making it seem like people from certain social groups must want to join certain ERGs?

12. **Declare your commitment to DEI.**

    a. What are some things your organization can do to declare its commitment to DEI?

    b. What must be done to make those declarations in ways that are authentic and not performative?

    c. Beyond declarations, what data can the organization reveal to describe its DEI journey, past, and goals?

13. **Ask for feedback.**

    a. What process can collect feedback from newly onboarding team members in ways that promote honesty and protect respondents from retribution?

    b. What questions would produce valuable onboarding feedback?

    c. How long would you wait until a new hire has joined the organization before approaching them for this feedback?

14. **Use feedback to help the organization evolve.**
    a. What process could be used to ask newcomers to provide feedback regarding how the organization can improve?
    b. What can be done to make potential respondents feel comfortable sharing these suggestions?
    c. What things can frame this feedback opportunity in a way that shows respondents the organization is committed to welcoming new ideas?

Chapter Seven: Retention

1. **Interrogate your retention plan.**
    a. Why would anyone want to stay with your organization?
    b. What does it do to encourage them to stay?
    c. What does it offer that others don't?

2. **Develop a formal retention plan.**
    a. What questions should appear in "stay interviews"?
    b. How does your organization use exit interviews?
    c. What other data could indicate the health of your retention plan?

3. **Provide inclusivity training.**
    a. What training does your organization provide?
    b. How does it create common language, values, and practices?
    c. Beyond achieving mere compliance, how does your training inspire enthusiastic support?

4. **Revise rules to be more inclusive.**
    a. What rules privilege which groups?
    b. How can they become more inclusive?
    c. Which rules must you retain for the benefit of all?

5. **Use flexible scheduling.**
   a. What does the data suggest about productivity and tele-commuting at your organization?
   b. Which tasks and positions could be remote?
   c. Beyond telecommuting, how else can your organization create more flexible scheduling?

6. **Create employee resource groups.**
   a. How can your organization improve employee resource groups?
   b. What policies can ensure they are supported but independent?
   c. What structures guarantee their recommendations for improvement are heard?

7. **Structure positive experiences.**
   a. What workday activities can increase positive experiences?
   b. What off-time activities can improve belonging?
   c. What other kinds of everyday micro-inclusions can overcome the deprivation effect?

8. **Support development.**
   a. What programs does your organization have to support development?
   b. What new ones could it develop?
   c. If your organization doesn't have the resources to support development, what other kinds of opportunities can it provide to help people learn, grow, and pursue passion projects?

9. **Provide a clear path to advancement.**
   a. What can your organization do to clarify the advancement process?

    b. If it doesn't have opportunities for promotion, what other things can it do to provide team members a sense of progress?

10. Retain like you're competing . . . because you already are!

    a. What are your competitors doing to retain people from underrepresented groups?

    b. What can your organization do to retain them that your competitors aren't doing?

    c. What processes are in place that can be used to ask team members what would retain them?

Chapter Eight: Mentoring

1. Develop structures that make intercultural mentorships possible.

    a. How can you invite people to volunteer for the mentorship program?

    b. How can you attract the greatest number of volunteers without pressuring them?

    c. How can you ensure invitations stand out and don't fade into the sea of other requests people receive?

2. Normalize mentorship as an essential part of professional development.

    a. How can you normalize mentorship?

    b. How can you overcome the stigma people might feel for seeking a mentor?

3. Reframe mentorships in terms of legacy.

    a. How can you appeal to a potential mentor's desire to leave a legacy?

b. Who at your organization feels this motivation?

c. What kind of value proposition would convince people interested in leaving a legacy to become mentors?

4. **Provide support.**

a. What funds could financially support mentorship programs?

b. What other kind of logistical support could your organization provide them?

c. What can the organization do to encourage participation in mentorship programs by making it as easy as possible for participants?

5. **Start with a cohort model.**

a. How often would your cohort meet?

b. How would you structure the meeting schedule?

c. How would you use this cohort time to diplomatically assess the ability of participants to be mentors?

6. **Provide training.**

a. What kind of training would you provide?

b. How would you train mentors on mentoring and mentees on how to self-advocate?

c. How would you create opportunities for mentors to learn from each and for mentees to do the same?

7. **Devote part of the mentoring time to project-based learning.**

a. How could you gather opinions about what kinds of projects to do?

b. How do you decide which projects are relevant and advantageous?

    c. How can you structure this portion of the mentorship so it seems professionally relevant without feeling like just extra work?

8. **Carefully create opportunities for pairings.**

    a. How could you diplomatically redirect people who want to mentor but might be better suited for other projects?

    b. How could you redirect people from mentorship pairings that might be disadvantageous?

    c. How do you balance the pairing committee's assessment with the desires of the mentors and mentees?

9. **Consider mentorships beyond your organization.**

    a. What other organizations could you partner with to create mentorships?

    b. What would you say to someone who worried that an inter-organizational mentorship program could lure mentees away from your organization?

    c. How can you ensure mentorships beyond your organization serve your team members well?

10. **Move beyond mentorship to sponsorship.**

    a. In your organization, who might be a good sponsor?

    b. How do you convince that person to become a sponsor?

    c. What can your organization do to support sponsors without micromanaging them?

11. **Become a mentor.**

    a. How can you become a mentor?

    b. What training would help you become a better mentor?

    c. What training would help you mentor across social identities?

12. **Become a mentee.**

    a. What mentorship opportunities exist for you to become a mentee?

    b. What opportunities exist for you to become a mentee to someone from a different social identity group?

    c. What can you do to ensure that your mentor from an under-represented group finds the mentorship rewarding rather than another instance where they have to educate someone on social issues that might be difficult?

Chapter Nine: Meetings

1. **Collect data.**

    a. What methods will work best for collecting data about your organization's meeting dynamics?

    b. How can that data be presented in ways that overcome defensiveness and lead to improvement?

    c. How can you collect data in ways that are accurate but not intrusive?

2. **Be intentional about scheduling.**

    a. When are meetings scheduled?

    b. Which groups are privileged by that scheduling? Which are disadvantaged by it?

    c. How can meetings be scheduled in more inclusive ways?

3. **Scrutinize where you hold meetings.**

    a. Where are meetings held?

    b. Which groups are privileged by those locations? Which are disadvantaged by them?

    c. How can meetings be located in more inclusive ways?

4. **Be strategic about your invitation list.**

   a. Who is essential to the meeting? How can you shrink the list of invitees to increase productivity? If there are a lot of people who need to meet, when is it time to split the single meeting with a lot of invitees into multiple smaller meetings with a few of them?

   b. Who is an outside voice that wouldn't be an obvious invitee but might provide unique and profound perspectives?

   c. If certain personalities dominate meetings and drown out others, what techniques can engage them in other ways that make it possible for them to miss meetings?

5. **Circulate the agenda ahead of time.**

   a. What are the specific questions people should come to the meeting having already thought about?

   b. What materials do invitees need in order to be informed?

   c. What other information can you cover beforehand so the meeting concentrates on collective problem solving?

6. **Share space.**

   a. How would round-robins work in your organization?

   b. What other conversational structures can give everyone the chance to talk without requiring everyone to do so?

   c. What structures can both share space and let ideas flow?

7. **Practice constructive dissent.**

   a. How can you structure dissent so it is required, expected, and productive?

   b. How can you encourage people to contradict themselves and explore multiple points of view on their own?

   c. How can you structure dissent in a way that goes beyond mere cynical contradiction to foster creative production?

8. **Return to the interrupted.**

   a. What will work best in your particular organization to stop interruptions but still accelerate conversation?

   b. How can you prevent interruptions before they happen?

   c. What is your script for returning to the interrupted?

   d. What is your script for when you've been interrupted?

9. **Keep credit where it's due.**

   a. Other than those provided in this chapter, what other tactics would you use to prevent idea repackaging before it happens?

   b. Once an incident of attempted idea theft has occurred, how would you ensure that credit for ideas remains with those who propose them?

   c. What is your script for ensuring you get credit for your ideas?

10. **Elevate ideas.**

   a. How can you elevate the ideas of others in a meeting?

   b. Who else do you know who might be interested in doing this during a meeting?

   c. How can you elevate the ideas of those who are often ignored without burying the ideas of those who often hold the floor?

11. **Follow up.**

   a. How detailed should meeting notes be? Who would take them?

   b. How soon after a meeting should they be circulated? What should be done with them?

   c. What information should meeting notes withhold?

12. **Share leadership.**

    a. What structures, systems, or "games" can help rotate who holds meetings?

    b. How can you give people who are often ignored in meetings the opportunity to lead them in ways that benefit everyone? What kind of information should you give to set them up for success?

    c. If someone doesn't want to lead a meeting, how can you give them a way out of doing so?

Chapter Ten: Performance Reviews

1. **Interrogate your current review process.**

    a. Who does reviews? Who gets reviewed? Why some and not others?

    b. What criteria are used to review people? Which social groups do those criteria favor? Which do they disadvantage? How can they be revised to be more inclusive? How do team members feel about the review process?

    c. How frequently do reviews take place? What can improve that frequency?

2. **Clarify scoring.**

    a. What scoring system does your review process use?

    b. How many numerical rating options would you need to provide enough nuance?

    c. What changes would clarify the explanation of numerical ratings?

3. **Require evidence.**

    a. What improvements to the review form can require more concrete evidence?

    b. How many pieces of evidence are enough to provide convincing support?

c. How many pieces of evidence are too much and will overwhelm people?

4. Structure criticism.

a. How would structuring criticism in terms of "accomplishments" and "goals" affect the review process at your organization?

b. How many accomplishments and goals should appear on reviews at your organization?

c. When you provide the same numbers of accomplishments and goals for every team member, there's the risk that underperforming team members won't realize how dire their situation might be. How can you give these employees the same number of goals as every other employee but still help them understand the severity of their situation enough to improve it?

5. Hold norming sessions.

a. Who should be invited to norming sessions?

b. How far in advance of reviews should they occur?

c. How would you take the results of these norming sessions between reviewers and share them with reviewees?

6. Lower the stakes.

a. How can your organization lower the stakes of reviews enough to help people be honest but ensure people still take them seriously enough for them to remain productive?

b. How frequently should your organization have reviews? At what point do reviews become too frequent? When are they not frequent enough?

c. How can your organization structure low-stakes check-ins so they maximize efficiency and accuracy by building one into the next until they culminate in large-scale annual reviews?

7. **Scaffold reviews.**

   a. How can the review process be scaffolded in ways that earn buy-in from reviewers because it is more efficient and saves them time?

   b. How can the review process be scaffolded in ways that earn buy-in from reviewees because it provides more clarity and opportunities to improve?

   c. How can the review process be scaffolded so it provides enough structure to transfer smoothly between multiple reviews, reviewers, and reviewees without becoming overly restrictive and stifling?

8. **Emphasize self-reflection.**

   a. If you had a form that reviewees had to complete for their self-reflection, what would it ask?

   b. How would those questions lead into the review process?

   c. How long should the document be? What other benchmarks should it have to complete?

9. **Make goals collaborative.**

   a. What steps can ensure the goals a reviewee creates match up to the review criteria and organizational goals?

   b. How would you push reviewees to go beyond proposing the goals they want in order to propose the goals that would actually be best for them? How will you know the difference between what goals are actually best for them and the ones you assume are?

   c. What criteria would ensure goals were specific, measurable, attainable, relevant, and time based enough?

10. **Increase transparency.**

    a. What internal workings of the review process could you reveal to the entire organization?

    b. For reasons of confidentiality, which would have to remain secret?

c. How could your organization disseminate this information?

11. **Decentralize decisions.**

   a. The traditional review process burdens reviewers with the task of trying to make enormous decisions without bias. Best practices note that the way to circumvent unconscious bias in decision-making is to bring in as many consciousnesses as possible, but this approach poses some complications. How can the review process be organized in a way that gives people the benefit of shared decision-making without feeling like they're being personally discredited?

   b. What processes can mitigate conflicts that could emerge between multiple reviewers?

   c. While decentralizing the decisions of any one decision maker, how can organizations also provide training to improve the equitable thinking of all decision makers?

12. **Propose 360-degree reviews.**

   a. How would your organization respond to 360-degree reviews? Why?

   b. What resistance do you anticipate? How can you address those concerns and earn support?

   c. Which specific leaders could you approach who might be willing to lead by example and pilot this practice?

Notes

INTRODUCTION

xiv **Constantly responding to the threat:** Agarwal, Pragya. (2020). *Sway: Unravelling Unconscious Bias*. Bloomsbury, 284.

xvi **Of course, the line between:** For example, one of the major calls for police reform is improved bias training, which would become a workplace issue requiring secured funding from administrators, buy-in from workers, and the participation of staff. Me Too movements might focus on sexual harassment and violence laws on a social level, but because many of these crimes happen in the workplace, they also become an issue of workplace policy. The constitutional protections secured by Obergefell v. Hodges also require HR changes for spousal benefits to cover same-sex partners.

xvii **For example, women constitute:** US Bureau of Labor Statistics. (January 22, 2021). "Table 3: Employment Status of the Civilian Noninstitutional Population by Age, Sex, and Race." In *Labor Force Statistics from the Current Population Survey* (2020). www.bls.gov/cps/cpsaat03.htm.

xvii **For stylistic reasons:** These terms have their problems. "Marginalized" might suggest hopeless and perpetual marginalization. "Minority" might be inaccurate, especially given the fact that many "minority" groups constitute a numerical majority. "Diverse" borders on grammatical fuzziness because usually it is only a group that has heterogeneous parts that can be diverse, and an individual person can be diverse only if they have heterogeneous parts within them.

xxi **Since June 2020:** Maurer, Roy. (August 6, 2020). "New DE&I Roles Spike after Racial Justice Protests." SHRM. www.shrm.org/resourcesandtools/hr-topics/talent-acquisition/pages/new-dei-roles-spike-after-racial-justice-protests.aspx.

xxi **For example, people increasingly want:** Maurer. "New DE&I Roles Spike."

xxi **More than ever, DEI:** Taplett, Frances Brooks, Garcia-Alonso, Jennifer, Krentz, Matt, & Poulsen, Mai-Britt. (March 5, 2020). "It's Frontline Leaders Who Make or Break Progress on Diversity." BCG. www.bcg.com/publications/2020/frontline-leaders-make-break-progress-diversity.

CHAPTER ONE: USE YOUR PRIVILEGE

5 **The most popular text regarding:** McIntosh, Peggy. (July/August 1989). "White Privilege: Unpacking the Invisible Knapsack." *Peace and Freedom.* https://psychology.umbc.edu/files/2016/10/White-Privilege_McIntosh -1989.pdf.

6–7 **Reductive definitions of White privilege:** Shrider, Emily A., Kollar, Melissa, Chen, Frances, & Semega, Jessica. (2021). *Income and Poverty in the United States: 2020.* US Census Bureau. www.census.gov/content/dam/Census/library /publications/2021/demo/p60-273.pdf.

16 **American adults identify as Christian:** Pew Research Center. (October 17, 2019). "In U.S., Decline of Christianity Continues at Rapid Pace." https:// www.pewforum.org/2019/10/17/in-u-s-decline-of-christianity-continues -at-rapid-pace.

Barna, George. (2001). *Growing True Disciples: New Strategies for Producing Genuine Followers of Christ.* Doubleday Religious.

21 **Regardless of your position:** Pavco-Giaccia, Olivia, Little, Martha Fitch, Stanley, Jason, & Dunham, Yarrow. (2019). "Rationality Is Gendered." *Collabra: Psychology, 5*(1), 54.

21 **For example, when women advocate:** Loyd, Denise Lewin, & Amoroso, Lisa M. (2018). "Undermining Diversity: Favoritism Threat and Its Effect on Advocacy for Similar Others." *Group Dynamics: Theory, Research, and Practice, 22*(3), 143–155.

22 **For example, calls:** Loyd & Amoroso. "Undermining Diversity."

CHAPTER TWO: CHECK YOURSELF

26 **career expert Alison Doyle compiles:** Doyle, Alison. (July 21, 2020). "Top 10 Reasons for Getting Fired." *The Balance Careers.* www.thebalancecareers.com /top-reasons-for-getting-fired-2060732.

28 **Gillian B. White shows:** White, Gillian B. (October 7, 2015). "Black Workers Really Do Need to Be Twice as Good." *The Atlantic.* www.theatlantic.com /business/archive/2015/10/why-black-workers-really-do-need-to-be-twice -as-good/409276/m.

28 **Black workers are more likely:** Cavounidis, Costas, & Lang, Kevin. (2015). "Discrimination and Worker Evaluation." Working Paper 21612. National Bureau of Economic Research. www.nber.org/system/files/working_papers /w21612/w21612.pdf.

29 **In *Sway: Unravelling Unconscious Bias:*** Agarwal, Pragya. (2020). *Sway: Unravelling Unconscious Bias.* Bloomsbury.

30 **According to the saying:** Crippen, Alex. (October 16, 2013). "Buffett on JP-Morgan: Jamie Dimon Will Survive Fine." CNBC. www.cnbc.com/2013/10/16 /buffett-on-jpmorgan-jamie-dimon-will-survive-fine.html. Interestingly, Warren Buffett said this quote to dismiss charges that JPMorgan Chase CEO Jamie Dimon misled investors regarding $6.2 billion in losses. This metaphor was used to describe the SEC surveillance of a billionaire's multibillion-dollar improprieties that ended up with his paying a settlement. It seems appropriate

to apply it to Black people who are actually policed for much longer with much more severe consequences.

32 **But that Dutch employee:** Meyer, Erin. (2014). *The Culture Map: Breaking through the Invisible Boundaries of Global Business.* PublicAffairs.

33 **people on the autism spectrum:** Oesch, Taryn. (August 19, 2019). "Autism at Work: Hiring and Training Employees on the Spectrum." SHRM. www.shrm.org/resourcesandtools/hr-topics/behavioral-competencies/global-and-cultural-effectiveness/pages/autism-at-work-hiring-and-training-employees-on-the-spectrum.aspx.

35 **That's the conclusion arrived at:** Wegner, Daniel M., Schneider, David J., Carter, Samuel R., & White, Teri L. (1987). "Paradoxical Effects of Thought Suppression." *Journal of Personality and Social Psychology, 53*(1), 5–13.

36 **focus on trying to not think:** Hertel, Paula T., & Calcaterra, Gina. (2005). "Intentional Forgetting Benefits from Thought Substitution." *Psychonomic Bulletin & Review, 12*(3), 484–489.

37 *StrengthsFinder 2.0* **is the only:** Kopf, Dan. (December 21, 2016). "Only One Book Has Made the Amazon Top 10 Every Year for the Past Decade." *Quartz.* https://qz.com/868736/strengthfinder-2-0-is-the-only-book-that-has-made-the-amazon-top-ten-every-year-for-the-last-decade.

The Economist. (June 30, 2011). "Busy, Busy." www.economist.com/books-and-arts/2011/06/30/busy-busy.

CHAPTER THREE: BUILD A BRIDGE

49 **finds that groups are 25:** Johnson, Stefanie K. (2020). *Inclusify: The Power of Uniqueness and Belonging to Build Innovative Teams.* Harper Business, x.

49 **About thirty-two million millennials:** Johnson. *Inclusify,* 61.

49 **In 2015, a McKinsey Global:** Woetzel, Jonathan, Madgavkar, Anu, Ellingrud, Kweilin, Labaye, Eric, Devillard, Sandrine, Kutcher, Eric, Manyika, James, Dobbs, Richard, & Krishnan, Mekala. (2015). *The Power of Parity: How Advancing Women's Equality Can Add $12 Trillion to Global Growth.* McKinsey Global Institute. www.mckinsey.com/featured-insights/employment-and-growth/how-advancing-womens-equality-can-add-12-trillion-to-global-growth.

49 **Finally, if banks more fairly lent:** Peterson, Dana M., Mann, Catherine L., & McGuire, Raymond J. (2020). *Closing the Racial Inequality Gaps: The Economic Cost of Black Inequality in the U.S.* https://eaccny.com/wp-content/uploads/2020/11/Citi-Closing-Racial-Inequality-Gaps-AX2QY.pdf.

49 **Beyond increased reach, inclusive organizations:** What to Become. (February 23, 2021). "The Importance of Diversity in the Workplace—20 Key Statistics." https://whattobecome.com/blog/diversity-in-the-workplace-statistics.

50 **The World Economic Forum projects:** Eswaran, Vijay. (April 29, 2019). "The Business Case for Diversity in the Workplace Is Now Overwhelming." World Economic Forum. www.weforum.org/agenda/2019/04/business-case-for-diversity-in-the-workplace.

50 **The 2020 Deloitte millennial survey:** Deloitte. (2020). "The Deloitte Global Millennial Survey 2020." Retrieved October 19, 2021, from https://www2.de

loitte.com/content/dam/Deloitte/global/Documents/About-Deloitte/de
loitte-2020-millennial-survey.pdf.

50 **Beyond attracting the most qualified:** Levine, Sheen S., Apfelbaum, Evan P.,
Bernard, Mark, Bartelt, Valerie L., Zajac, Edward J., & Stark, David. (2014).
"Ethnic Diversity Deflates Price Bubbles." *PNAS, 111*(52), 18524–18529.

50 **It helps mitigate biases:** Cox, Christine, Rock, David, & Grant, Heidi. (2021).
"Breaking Bias Updated: The Seeds Model." NeuroLeadership Institute. https://
membership.neuroleadership.com/material/breaking-bias-updated-the
-seeds-model.

50 **With greater inclusion, teams are:** Phillips, Katherine W., Liljenquist, Katie
A., & Neale, Margaret A. (2008). "Is the Pain Worth the Gain? The Advantages
and Liabilities of Agreeing with Socially Distinct Newcomers." *Personality
and Social Psychology Bulletin, 35*(3), 336–350. https://doi.org/10.1177/0146167
208328062.

50 **While members of homogeneous:** Díaz-García, Cristina, González-Moreno,
Angela, & Sáez-Martínez, Francisco Jose. (2013). "Gender Diversity within
R&D Teams: Its Impact on Radicalness of Innovation." *Innovation, 15*(2),
149–160.

50 **A recent Edelman:** Edelman. (2020). *Special Report: Brand Trust in 2020:
Edelman Trust Barometer 2020.* www.edelman.com/sites/g/files/aatuss191
/files/2020-06/2020%20Edelman%20Trust%20Barometer%20Specl%20
Rept%20Brand%20Trust%20in%202020.pdf.

51 **With more than half:** Desai, Rupen. (October 3, 2018). "It's Time for the Bar-
code to Carry a Moral Code." Edelman. www.edelman.com/post/its-time-for
-the-barcode-to-carry-moral-code.

51 **Inclusive companies increase:** What to Become. "The Importance of Diversity in the Workplace."

51 **For example, when NFL:** Thorson, Emily A., & Serazio, Michael. (2018).
"Sports Fandom and Political Attitudes." *Public Opinion Quarterly, 82*(2),
391–403.

Nielsen. (July 2020). "Sports Fans Over-Index In Support of Blacks Lives
Matter Movement." www.nielsen.com/wp-content/uploads/sites/3/2020/07
/nielsen-sports-blm-Infographic.pdf.

51 **The reluctant point:** Solender, Andrew. (April 26, 2021). "'Get Woke. Go
Broke': GOP Calls Grow to Punish 'Woke' Businesses with Legislation." *Forbes.*
www.forbes.com/sites/andrewsolender/2021/04/26/get-woke-go-broke-gop
-calls-grow-to-punish-woke-businesses-with-legislation/?sh=6c8699651fac.

52 **In "Who Actually Boycotts Brands?":** Zara, Christopher. (September 20,
2019). "Who Actually Boycotts Brands? More Liberals and College Grads, It
Turns Out." *Fast Company.* www.fastcompany.com/90407051/who-boycotts
-brands-liberals-and-college-grads-says-study.

52 **Gun buyers vowed:** Ordabayeva, Nailya. (June 19, 2018). "How Liberals and
Conservatives Shop Differently." *Harvard Business Review.* https://hbr.org
/2018/06/how-liberals-and-conservatives-shop-differently.

52 **Despite the promise:** Associated Press. (February 13, 2021). "Forget 'Go
Woke, Go Broke,' NASCAR Claims Social Justice Is at Forefront as New Sea-
son Begins." Associated Press. https://www.marketwatch.com/story/forget-go

-woke-go-broke-nascar-claims-social-justice-is-at-forefront-as-new-season
-begins-01613256790.

53 **While it's difficult:** CIM. (February 3, 2020). "When Brands Go Woke, Do They Go Broke?" www.cim.co.uk/content-hub/editorial/when-brands-go-woke -do-they-go-broke.

55 **But the second:** Kaplan, Sarah. (February 12, 2020). "Why the 'Business Case' for Diversity Isn't Working." *Fast Company.* https://www.fastcompany.com /90462867/why-the-business-case-for-diversity-isnt-working.

55 **Economist Robin J. Ely:** Ely, Robin J., & Thomas, David A. (November–December 2020). "Getting Serious about Diversity: Enough Already with the Business Case, It's Time for a New Way of Thinking." *Harvard Business Review.* https://hbr.org/2020/11/getting-serious-about-diversity-enough-already -with-the-business-case.

60 **the "hypocrisy paradigm" emphasizes:** Gawronski, Bertram, & Stack, Fritz. (Eds.). (2012). *Cognitive Consistency: A Fundamental Principle in Social Cognition.* Guilford Press, 10.

61 **A study of hundreds:** Lucidity. (2021). "The Top Ten Most Common Company Values." Lucidity. https://getlucidity.com/strategy-resources/top-ten-most -common-company-values.

CHAPTER FOUR: RECRUITING

71 **It is not Hampten:** Glassdoor Team. (July 12, 2021). "What Job Seekers Really Think About Your Diversity and Inclusion Stats." Glassdoor for Employers. www.glassdoor.com/employers/blog/diversity.

71 **It is not students:** Lorenzo, Rocío, Voigt, Nicole, Tsusaka, Miki, Krentz, Matt, & Abouzahr, Katie. (January 23, 2018). "How Diverse Leadership Teams Boost Innovation." Boston Consulting Group. https://www.bcg.com/publica tions/2018/how-diverse-leadership-teams-boost-innovation.

71 **One might feel:** Peterson, Dana M., Mann, Catherine L., & McGuire, Raymond J. (2020). *Closing the Racial Inequality Gaps: The Economic Cost of Black Inequality in the U.S.* https://eaccny.com/wp-content/uploads/2020/11/Citi -Closing-Racial-Inequality-Gaps-AX2QY.pdf.

74 **Studies show that biased:** Gaucher, Danielle, Friesen, Justin, & Kay, Aaron C. (2011). "Evidence That Gendered Wording in Job Advertisements Exists and Sustains Gender Inequality." *Journal of Personality and Social Psychology,* *101*(1), 109–128.

75 **Resist the tendency:** Helpful resources to start screening your job ads for biased terms include Gender Decoder, Textio, and Applied.

75 **Psychologists Jessi L. Smith:** Smith, Jessi L., & Huntoon, Meghan. (2014). "Women's Bragging Rights: Overcoming Modesty Norms to Facilitate Women's Self-Promotion." *Psychology of Women Quarterly,* 38(4), 447–459.

76 **Nancy F. Clark:** Clark, Nancy F. (April 28, 2014). "Act Now to Shrink the Confidence Gap." *Forbes.* www.forbes.com/sites/womensmedia/2014/04/28 /act-now-to-shrink-the-confidence-gap/?sh=bbcc8b45c41c.

76 **From this data:** Mohr, Tara Sophia. (August 25, 2014). "Why Women Don't Apply for Jobs Unless They're 100% Qualified." *Harvard Business Review.*

https://hbr.org/2014/08/why-women-dont-apply-for-jobs-unless-theyre-100 -qualified.

76 **Suspecting the professional:** Clance, Pauline R., & Imes, Suzanne A. (1978). "The Impostor Phenomenon in High Achieving Women: Dynamics and Therapeutic Intervention." *Psychotherapy: Theory, Research & Practice, 15*(3), 241–247.

   Walton, Gregory M., & Cohen, Geoffrey L. (2007). "A Question of Belonging: Race, Social Fit, and Achievement." *Journal of Personality and Social Psychology, 92*(1), 82–96.

78 **Partner with university:** Rakuna. (2018). "13 Innovative Best Practice Strategies to Diversity Recruiting." Retrieved November 30, 2021, from www.rakuna .co/blog/posts/diversity-recruiting-strategy-best-practices.

CHAPTER FIVE: HIRING

84 **In *The Psychology of Behaviour*:** Furnham, Adrian. (2005). *The Psychology of Behaviour at Work: The Individual in the Organization.* Psychology Press, 116.

84 **Experimental psychologist and chief psychometrician:** Birwadker, Samar. (April 10, 2015). "Culture Fit in the Workplace: What It Is and Why It's Important." https://www.linkedin.com/pulse/culture-fit-workplace-what-why-its -important-samar-birwadker.

84 **Bailey Reiners argues:** Reiners, Bailey. (April 12, 2021). "Culture Fit: More Harm Than Good? 12 Experts Share Their Take." Built In. https://builtin .com/company-culture/cultural-fit.

87 **When facing those who argue:** Many in this industry call this approach "blind auditions." To avoid possibly ableist language, I'll use "redacted" or "anonymized."

87 **GapJumpers found that when employers:** Cooper, Marianne. (December 1, 2015). "The False Promise of Meritocracy." *The Atlantic.* https://www.the atlantic.com/business/archive/2015/12/meritocracy/418074.

88 **Korn Ferry reports:** Mulrooney, Byrne, Mueller, Jan, & Gilbert, Bill. "The Talent Forecast: Hire with a Purpose." Retrieved December 2, 2021, from https://www.kornferry.com/insights/this-week-in-leadership/the-talent -forecast-hire-with-a-purpose.

88 **In 2018, 91 percent:** Entelo. (2018). *Entelo 2018 Recruiting Trends Report.*

89 **Because no matter how objective:** Agarwal, Pragya. (2020). *Sway: Unravelling Unconscious Bias.* Bloomsbury, 366–367.

91 **Interestingly, when companies:** Johnson, Stefanie K. (2020). *Inclusify: The Power of Uniqueness and Belonging to Build Innovative Teams.* Harper Business, 25.

94 **Seeing past buzzwords:** Maurer, Roy. (April 17, 2018). "Ditch the 'Beer Test' and Start Hiring for Culture Add." SHRM. www.shrm.org/resourcesandtools /hr-topics/talent-acquisition/pages/ditch-the-beer-test-and-start-hiring-for -culture-add.aspx.

95 **In the end, she:** Pager, Devah. (2003). "The Mark of a Criminal Record." *American Journal of Sociology, 108*(5), 937–975.

96 **They conclude that this:** Goldin, Claudia, & Rouse, Cecilia. (2000). "Orchestrating Impartiality: The Impact of 'Blind' Auditions on Female Musicians." *American Economic Review, 90*(4), 715–741.

97 **Beyond being able to identify:** Johnson. *Inclusify,* 67.

97 **passive transparency is:** Johnson. *Inclusify,* 69.

99 **As Galinsky claims:** Galinsky, Adam D., Todd, Andrew R., Homan, Astrid C., Phillips, Katherine W., Apfelbaum, Evan P., Sasaki, Stacey J., Richeson, Jennifer A., Olayon, Jennifer B., & Maddux, William W. (2015). "Maximizing the Gains and Minimizing the Pains of Diversity: A Policy Perspective." *Perspectives on Psychological Science, 10*(6), 742–748.

100 **In short, Jansen:** Jansen, Wiebren S., Otten, Sabine, & van der Zee, Karen I. (2015). "Being Part of Diversity: The Effects of an All-Inclusive Multicultural Diversity Approach on Majority Members' Perceived Inclusion and Support for Organizational Diversity Efforts." *Group Processes & Intergroup Relations, 18*(6), 817–832.

102 **In a strange twist:** Of course, enormous problems still remain with managing bias by anonymizing and redacting the hiring process. For starters, it works in some contexts and not necessarily in others (Behaghel, Luc, Crépon, Bruno, & Le Barbanchon, Thomas. [2014]. "Unintended Effects of Anonymous Resumes." IZA DP No. 8517. IZA Paper Discussion Series. IZA. http://ftp.iza .org/dp8517.pdf). Also, it can sidestep the problem of exclusion by ignoring difference instead of recognizing difference as a virtue (Maurer, Roy [February 4, 2016]. "Blind Hiring May Be Missing the Point. SHRM. www.shrm.org /resourcesandtools/hr-topics/talent-acquisition/pages/blind-hiring-practices .aspx). Perhaps the biggest problem with anonymized hiring practices is that they don't do the prework of making a more inclusive company culture. These practices can leave open the possibility that a revamped process hires more diverse talent but ends up subjecting those new hires to countless microaggressions, tokenism, and biases because the organization hasn't done the work of making itself a more inclusive place that has room for people hired from underrepresented communities. To address these issues, chapter six goes beyond simply getting people in the door through diversity hiring to making sure that, once they enter, there's room for them at the table.

CHAPTER SIX: ONBOARDING

105 **It refers to the process:** Maurer, Roy. (n.d.). "New Employee Onboarding Guide." SHRM. Retrieved December 3, 2021, from www.shrm.org/resource sandtools/hr-topics/talent-acquisition/pages/new-employee-onboarding -guide.aspx.

105 **According to a Society:** Bauer, Talya N. (2010). "Onboarding New Employees: Maximizing Success." *SHRM Foundation's Effective Practice Guidelines Series.* SHRM. www.shrm.org/foundation/ourwork/initiatives/resources-from -past-initiatives/Documents/Onboarding%20New%20Employees.pdf.

105 **In 2009, an Aberdeen Group:** Maurer, Roy. (April 16, 2015). "Onboarding Key to Retaining, Engaging Talent." SHRM. www.shrm.org/resourcesandtools

/hr-topics/talent-acquisition/pages/onboarding-key-retaining-engaging-talent.aspx.

105 **These companies concentrate:** Bauer. "Onboarding New Employees."

106 **In the workplace, people:** Paludi, Michael A. (Ed.). (2012). *Managing Diversity in Today's Workplace: Strategies for Employees and Employers.* Praeger.

    Sue, Derald W., Capodilupo, Christina M., Torino, Gina C., Bucceri, Jennifer M., Holder, Aisha M. B., Nadal, Kevin L., & Esquilin, Marta. (2007). "Racial Microaggressions in Everyday Life: Implications for Clinical Practice." *The American Psychologist, 62*(4), 271–286. https://doi.org10.1037/0003-066X.62.4.271.

    Basford, Tess E., Offermann, Lynn R., & Behrend, Tara S. (November 19, 2013). "Do You See What I See? Perceptions of Gender Microaggressions in the Workplace." *Psychology of Women Quarterly, 38*(3), 340–349.

107 **In the end, people:** Rozovsky, Julia. (November 17, 2015). "The Five Keys to a Successful Google Team." Re:Work. https://rework.withgoogle.com/blog/five-keys-to-a-successful-google-team.

108 **They structure this process:** Dewar, Jen. (July 5, 2021). "Top Employee Onboarding Programs." Sapling. www.saplinghr.com/top-employee-onboarding-programs#3.

108 **In addition to the internal:** Cordivano, Sarah. (December 17, 2019). "Understanding and Designing an Inclusive Onboarding Experience." Medium. https://medium.com/sarah-cordivano/understanding-and-designing-an-inclusive-onboarding-experience-4be6b5f7c669.

109 **According to chief diversity:** Gordon, Stacey A. (June 16, 2020). "Inclusive Onboarding: How the Right Onboarding Team Can Help You Retain Top Talent." Breezy. https://breezy.hr/blog/inclusive-onboarding.

110 **For this reason, put:** Trinidad, Ciara. (May 9, 2017). "Creating an Inclusive Onboarding Experience." Lever. www.lever.co/blog/a-step-by-step-guide-to-cultivating-diversity-and-inclusion-part-8-after-the-hire.

111 **For them, there's:** Indeed. (January 3, 2021). "New Hire Onboarding Checklist." www.indeed.com/hire/c/info/new-hire-onboarding-checklist?aceid=&gclid=EAIaIQobChMIsbLK55i98AIVBG1vBB1D_QFLEAAYAyAAEgJGJ_D_BwE.

111 **Have an anti-discrimination:** Cordivano. "Understanding and Designing an Inclusive Onboarding Experience."

113 **According to applied social:** Gruman, Jamie A., & Saks, Alan M. (2018). "E-Socialization: The Problems and the Promise of Socializing Newcomers in the Digital Age." In James H. Dulebohn & Dianna L. Stone (Eds.), *Research in Human Resource Management: The Brave New World of eHRM 2.0.* IAP Information Age, 111–139.

113 **In fact, one study found:** Aberdeen. (September 22, 2016). "Perfecting the Onboarding Funnel." www.aberdeen.com/hcm-essentials/perfecting-onboarding-funnel.

113 **According to HR business:** Pavlina, Kaitlyn. (2020). Assessing Best Practices for the Virtual Onboarding of New Technology Industry. (Publication No. 1168) [Master's thesis, Pepperdine University]. Pepperdine Digital Commons, 24. https://digitalcommons.pepperdine.edu/cgi/viewcontent.cgi?article=2167&context=etd.

114 **Share enough information:** Benson Executive Search. (n.d.). "Driving and Reinforcing a Strong DEI Culture: Onboarding." Retrieved December 3, 2021, from www.bensonsearch.com/blog/2020/8/25/driving-and-reinforcing-a-strong-dei-culture-onboarding.

115 **He notes, "If someone":** Przystanski, Andy. (August 3, 2020). "4 Tips for Making Employee Onboarding More Inclusive." Lattice. https://lattice.com/library/4-tips-for-making-employee-onboarding-more-inclusive.

116 **Many employers use:** Sue et al. "Racial Microaggressions in Everyday Life."

CHAPTER SEVEN: RETENTION

123 **In "Companies Need":** Conerly, Bill. (August 12, 2018). "Companies Need to Know the Dollar Cost of Employee Turnover." *Forbes.* www.forbes.com/sites/billconerly/2018/08/12/companies-need-to-know-the-dollar-cost-of-employee-turnover/?sh=623a8527d590.

126 **For this, conduct:** Santos, Marcelle. (July 9, 2020). "9 Ways to Retain Diverse Talent." TextExpander. https://textexpander.com/blog/9-ways-to-retain-diverse-talent.

126 **What can I do:** Finnegan, Richard. "How to Conduct Stay Interviews: 5 Key Questions: Part 2." *The Power of Stay Interviews for Engagement and Retention.* SHRM. www.shrm.org/resourcesandtools/hr-topics/employee-relations/pages/how-to-conduct-stay-interviews-part-2.aspx.

127 **When diverse employees:** Santos. "9 Ways to Retain Diverse Talent."

128 **In a survey of 540:** Heinig, Ian. (February 20, 2019). "How Do Employees Act When Faced with Unethical Company Behavior?" The Manifest. https://themanifest.com/business-services/how-employees-respond-unethical-company-behavior.

130 **These looser structures:** US Department of Labor. "Flexible Work Arrangements." Office of Disability Employment Policy. www.dol.gov/agencies/odep/program-areas/employment-supports/flexible-work-arrangements.

130 **According to the National:** National Council on Disability. (July 26, 2007). *Implementation of the Americans with Disabilities Act: Challenges, Best Practices, and New Opportunities for Success.* https://ncd.gov/publications/2007/july262007.

131 **In "Building an Inclusive":** Engers, Abby. "Building an Inclusive Workplace: Six Ways to Retain Diverse Talent." Mac's List. www.macslist.org/for-employers/building-an-inclusive-workplace-six-ways-to-retain-diverse-talent.

131 **According to retention consultant:** Lassiter, Pam. (n.d.). "Flexibility In The Workplace And Why It Matters." Monster. Retrieved December 3, 2021, from https://hiring.monster.com/employer-resources/workforce-management/employee-performance/employee-engagement-ideas.

134 **Results revealed marginalized:** Norlander, Peter, Does, Serena, & Shih, Margaret. (2020). "Deprivation at Work: Positive Workplace Experiences and the Racial Gap in Quit Intentions." https://anderson-review.ucla.edu/wp-content/uploads/2021/03/Norlander-Does-Shih_Positive_Empirical_Anderson_Review.pdf.

134 **This research encourages:** Norlander et al. "Deprivation at Work," 24.

136 **many respondents went on:** LinkedIn Learning. (2018). *2018 Workplace Learning Report: The Rise and Responsibility of Talent Development in the New Labor Market.* LinkedIn, 26. https://learning.linkedin.com/content/dam/me /learning/en-us/pdfs/linkedin-learning-workplace-learning-report-2018.pdf.

137 **Forty-two percent sought:** Catalyst. (2003). "Women in U.S. Corporate Leadership," 6. https://www.catalyst.org/wp-content/uploads/2019/01/Women_in _US_Corporate_Leadership.pdf.

138 **Fifty-seven percent of employees:** What to Become. (February 23, 2021). "The Importance of Diversity in the Workplace—20 Key Statistics." https://what tobecome.com/blog/diversity-in-the-workplace-statistics.

139 **For example, if you adopt:** Engers. "Building an Inclusive Workplace."

139 **Point out that voluntary:** McFeely, Shane, & Wigert, Ben. (March 13, 2019). "This Fixable Problem Costs U.S. Businesses $1 Trillion." Gallup. www.gallup .com/workplace/247391/fixable-problem-costs-businesses-trillion.aspx.

CHAPTER EIGHT: MENTORING

143 **"another way to engage managers":** Dobbin, Frank, & Kalev, Alexandra. (July–August 2016). "Why Diversity Programs Fail: And What Works Better." *Harvard Business Review.* https://hbr.org/2016/07/why-diversity-programs-fail.

144 **These programs diversify:** Dobbin & Kalev. "Why Diversity Programs Fail."

144 **In a six-year period:** Dobbin & Kalev.

144 **The hard work of diverse:** Murrell, Audrey J., Crosby, Faye J., & Ely, Robin J. (Eds.). (1999). *Mentoring Dilemmas: Developmental Relationships within Multicultural Organizations.* Lawrence Erlbaum Associates.

Blake-Beard, Stacy D., Murrell, Audrey J., & Thomas, David. (2007). "Unfinished Business: The Impact of Race on Understanding Mentoring Relationships." In Belle Rose Ragins & Kathy E. Kram (Eds.), *The Handbook of Mentoring at Work: Theory, Research, and Practice.* Sage, 223–248.

Thomas, David A., & Gabarro, John J. (1999). *Breaking Through: The Making of Minority Executives in Corporate America.* Harvard Business School Press.

146 **Society tells them:** Walton, Gregory M., & Cohen, Geoffrey L. (2007). "A Question of Belonging: Race, Social Fit, and Achievement." *Journal of Personality and Social Psychology, 92*(1), 82–96.

146 **To succeed in:** Cokley, Kevin, McClain, Shannon, Enciso, Alicia, & Martinez, Mercedes. (2013). "An Examination of the Impact of Minority Status Stress and Impostor Feelings on the Mental Health of Diverse Ethnic Minority College Students." *Journal of Multicultural Counseling and Development, 41*(2), 82–95.

146 **This extraordinary pressure:** Miller, Darlene G., & Kastberg, Signe M. (1995). "Of Blue Collars and Ivory Towers: Women from Blue-Collar Backgrounds in Higher Education." *Roeper Review, 18*(1), 27–33.

148 **According to her, "these nominees":** Mason, Kate. (n.d.). "Won't You Be My Mentor? 5 Strategies for Convincing Your Top-Tier Employees to Participate." eMentorConnect. Retrieved December 3, 2021, from https://ementorconnect .com/wont-mentor-5-strategies-convincing-top-tier-employees-participate.

154 **According to a study led:** Murrell, Audrey J., Blake-Beard, Stacy, Porter, David M., Jr., & Perkins-Williamson, Addie. (2008). "Interorganizational Formal Mentoring: Breaking the Concrete Ceiling Sometimes Requires Support from the Outside." *Human Resource Management*, 47(2), 275–294. https://doi -org.marianuniversity.idm.oclc.org/10.1002/hrm.20212.

154 **They define this concept:** Murrell et al. "Interorganizational Formal Mentoring."

155 **Ultimately, even when:** Murrell et al.

156 **They call in favors:** Coqual. (2019). *The Sponsor Dividend: Key Findings*. https://coqual.org/wp-content/uploads/2020/09/CoqualTheSponsorDivi dend_KeyFindingsCombined090720.pdf.

CHAPTER NINE: MEETINGS

163 **In 2016, professor of global:** Cross, Rob, Rebele, Reb, & Grant, Adam. (January–February 2016). "Collaborative Overload." *Harvard Business Review*. https://hbr.org/2016/01/collaborative-overload.

163 **That same year, journalist:** Heffernan, Virginia. (February 25, 2016). "Meet Is Murder." *The New York Times Magazine*. www.nytimes.com/2016/02/28 /magazine/meet-is-murder.html.

163 **During the COVID-19:** Kost, Danielle. (September 14, 2020). "You're Right! You Are Working Longer and Attending More Meetings." *Working Knowledge*. https://hbswk.hbs.edu/item/you-re-right-you-are-working-longer-and -attending-more-meetings.

163 **Kauffeld and Nale Lehmann-Willenbrock analyzed:** Kauffeld, Simone, & Lehmann-Willenbrock, Nale. (2012). "Meetings Matter: Effects of Team Meetings on Team and Organizational Success." *Small Group Research*, 43(2), 130–158.

164 **Female executives who talk:** Brescoll, Victoria L. (2011). "Who Takes the Floor and Why: Gender, Power, and Volubility in Organizations." *Administrative Science Quarterly*, 56(4), 622–641.

164 **Award-winning psychologist Dolly Chugh claims:** Chugh, Dolly. (October 20, 2020). "How to Have More Inclusive Meetings over Zoom." Ideas.Ted .Com. https://ideas.ted.com/how-to-have-inclusive-meetings-over-zoom.

165 **In a study of 360-degree feedback:** Heath, Kathryn, & Wensil, Brenda F. (September 6, 2019). "To Build an Inclusive Culture, Start with Inclusive Meetings." *Harvard Business Review*. https://hbr.org/2019/09/to-build-an-inclusive-culture -start-with-inclusive-meetings.

166 **They try to determine:** These discrete technologies can be a valuable tool for starting to look at numbers, but they have limitations. To begin with, they make assumptions about gender based on the voices of speakers, which assumes deep voices belong to men and higher ones to women. For this reason, these apps can fail to account for men with higher voices, women with deeper ones, people who identify as transgender, and people who identify as nonbinary.

169 **Encourage their participation:** Greesonbach, Sarah. (August 3, 2020). "5 Ways to Run More Inclusive Meetings." Glassdoor. www.glassdoor.com/em ployers/blog/run-more-inclusive-meetings.

170 **"list agenda items as questions"**: Atlassian. (2021). "Inclusive Meetings." www.atlassian.com/team-playbook/plays/inclusive-meetings.

172 **They found that group intelligence:** Woolley, Anita Williams, Chabris, Christopher F., Pentland, Alex, Hashmi, Nada, & Malone, Thomas W. (2010). "Evidence for a Collective Intelligence Factor in the Performance of Human Groups." *Science, 330*(6004), 686–688. www.cs.cmu.edu/~ab/Salon/research /Woolley_et_al_Science_2010-2.pdf.

176 **Conversely, when the tables:** Brescoll. "Who Takes the Floor and Why."

177 **leaders who interrupt:** Farley, Sally D. (2008). "Attaining Status at the Expense of Likeability: Pilfering Power through Conversational Interruption." *Journal of Nonverbal Behavior, 32*(4), 241–260.

177 **Among them are to let:** Monarth, Harrison. (June 23, 2021). "How to Manage Interruptions in Meetings." *Harvard Business Review.* https://hbr.org/2021/06 /how-to-manage-interruptions-in-meetings.

177 **While many interrupt people:** While working against interruption, keep in mind that many different ethnicities also practice "cooperative overlapping." In some groups, it seems rude to cut off speakers. In others, if you let people finish, you might seem uninterested. Borresen, Kelsey. (March 4, 2021). "How to Know If You're an Interrupter or a 'Cooperative Overlapper.'" *HuffPost.* www.huffpost.com/entry/interrupting-or-cooperative-overlapping_1 _603e8ae9c5b601179ec0ff4e.

178 **They found most women:** Heath, Kathryn, Flynn, Jill, & Holt, Mary Davis. (June 2014). "Women, Find Your Voice." *Harvard Business Review.* https:// hbr.org/2014/06/women-find-your-voice.

CHAPTER TEN: PERFORMANCE REVIEWS

185 **In studies that have looked:** Mount, Michael K., Judge, Timothy A., Scullen, Steven E., Sytsma, Marcia R., & Hezlett, Sarah A. (1998). "Trait, Rater and Level Effects in 360-Degree Performance Ratings." *Personnel Psychology, 51*(3), 557–576.

Scullen, Steven E., Mount, Michael K., & Goff, Maynard. (2000). "Understanding the Latent Structure of Job Performance Ratings." *Journal of Applied Psychology, 85*(6), 956–970.

Hoffman, Brian, Lance, Charles E., Bynum, Bethany, & Gentry, William A. (2010). "Rater Source Effects Are Alive and Well After All." *Personnel Psychology, 63*(1), 119–151.

185 **According to business consultant:** Buckingham, Marcus. (February 9, 2015). "Most HR Data Is Bad Data." *Harvard Business Review.* https://hbr.org/2015 /02/most-hr-data-is-bad-data.

186 **Regardless of the reviewer's race or ethnicity:** Reeves, Arin N. (2014). "Written in Black & White: Exploring Confirmation Bias in Racialized Perceptions of Writing Skills." Nextions. http://nextions.com/wp-content/uploads/2017 /05/written-in-black-and-white-yellow-paper-series.pdf.

186 **Joan C. Williams, Denise Lewin Loyd:** Williams, Joan C., Loyd, Denise Lewin, Boginsky, Mikayla, & Armas-Edwards, Frances. (April 21, 2021). "How One Company Worked to Root Out Bias from Performance Reviews."

Harvard Business Review. https://hbr.org/2021/04/how-one-company-worked-to-root-out-bias-from-performance-reviews.

186 **According to Melissa Phillippi:** Phillippi, Melissa. (April 16, 2019). "Overcoming Challenges of the Idiosyncratic Rater Effect." Performance Culture. https://performanceculture.com/overcoming-challenges-of-rater-bias/.

187 **Ratings might privilege:** Wiles, Jackie. (August 15, 2019). "The Real Impact on Employees of Removing Performance Ratings." Gartner. www.gartner.com/smarterwithgartner/corporate-hr-removing-performance-ratings-is-unlikely-to-improve-performance.

191 **Conversely, spending most:** Walton, Gregory M., & Cohen, Geoffrey L. (2007). "A Question of Belonging: Race, Social Fit, and Achievement." *Journal of Personality and Social Psychology, 92*(1), 82–96.

194 **Peter Cappelli and Anna Tavis:** Cappelli, Peter, & Tavis, Anna. (October 2016). "The Performance Management Revolution." *Harvard Business Review.* https://hbr.org/2016/10/the-performance-management-revolution.

196 **Most organizations have:** BambooHR. (n.d.). "An HR Glossary for HR Terms." Retrieved December 4, 2021, from www.bamboohr.com/hr-glossary/performance-review.

196 **In the form of self-reviews:** AllBusiness. (May 20, 2008). "The Benefits of Employee Self-Reviews." *The New York Times.* https://archive.nytimes.com/www.nytimes.com/allbusiness/AB10175081_primary.html.

197 **The Corporate Leadership Council's global:** Corporate Leadership Council. (2004). "Driving Performance and Retention through Employee Engagement: Executive Summary," 4. www.stcloudstate.edu/humanresources/_files/documents/supv-brown-bag/employee-engagement.pdf.

197 **According to Michael Henckel:** Henckel, Michael. (May 23, 2017). "How Self-Assessments Can Strengthen Your Annual Review Process." *The Business Journals.* www.bizjournals.com/bizjournals/how-to/human-resources/2017/05/how-self-assessments-can-strengthen-your-annual.html.

198 **more likely to achieve them:** Schraeder, Mike, Becton, J. Bret, & Portis, Ron. (March 2007). "A Critical Examination of Performance Appraisals: An Organization's Friend or Foe?" *The Journal for Quality and Participation, 30*(1), 20–25.

199 **To overcome all these issues:** Illig, Randy. (October 23, 2018). "A High-Trust Sales Organization Starts From The Top." *Forbes.* https://www.forbes.com/sites/randyillig/2018/10/23/a-high-trust-sales-organization-starts-from-the-top/?sh=3e6565524af9.

CHAPTER ELEVEN: NEXT STEPS

214 **In "Managing the Toll":** Carter, Kevin. (February 27, 2020). "Managing the Toll of DEI Work: The Physiology of Inclusion." *The Inclusion Solution.* www.theinclusionsolution.me/managing-the-toll-of-dei-work-the-physiology-of-inclusion.

215 **For some that may seem:** Clarey, Katie. (November 11, 2019). "How to Get Middle Managers to Commit to D&I—Even When They Don't Want To." *HR Dive.* www.hrdive.com/news/how-to-get-middle-managers-to-commit-to-di-even-when-they-dont-want-to-1/567029.

Index